Yellow Fax and Other Poems

Agincourt Books are edited and published by

Luigi Ballerini
Beppe Cavatorta
Gianluca Rizzo
Federica Santini

All rights reserved.

ISBN: 978-1-946328-21-2

AGINCOURT PRESS
P.O. Box 1039
Cooper Station
New York, NY 10003
www.agincourtpress.org

©1993, 1994, and 2000 by Mariano Bàino
© 2019 English edition by Agincourt Press

The publisher welcomes enquiries from copyright-holders he has been unable to contact

Mariano Bàino

Yellow Fax and Other Poems

*Edited and with an Introduction by
Gianluca Rizzo*

*Translated by
Dominic Siracusa and Gianluca Rizzo*

Agincourt Press
New York, 2019

Table of Contents

7 Gianluca Rizzo
Language, Politics, and the Third Wave of Avantgarde: An Introduction to Mariano Báino's Poetry

36 FAX GIALLO
37 YELLOW FAX

80 Da ÔNNE 'E TERRA
81 From LAND WAVES

158 da PINOCCHIO (MOVIOLE)
159 From PINOCCHIO (REPLAYS)

Gianluca Rizzo

Language, Politics, and the Third Wave of Avantgarde: An Introduction to the Poetry of Mariano Bàino[1]

Mariano Bàino's is among the most interesting poetry to be published at the end of last century; it is constantly straddling the border between different linguistic codes and is capable of reaching the reader without compromising the complexity of its experimentation, continuing a tradition whose immediate predecessors are the neo-avant-garde of Novissimi and Gruppo 63. This introduction will situate Bàino, as well as his fellow members of Gruppo 93, within the recent history of Italian literature and offer a few remarks on three of his most interesting books of verse: *Fax giallo*, *Ônne 'e terra*, and *Pinocchio (moviole)*.[2]

We will begin with the aftermath of the disbandment of Gruppo 63, a crucial moment for the Italian poetry of the second half of the Twentieth Century. Here is a brief quotation, from the "Preface" to the volume *Terza Ondata: Il Nuovo Movimento della Scrittura in Italia* (edited by Bettini and Di Marco), that describes the origins of the name "Gruppo 93," its ties to Gruppo 63, and the atmosphere that surrounded the birth of the former:

> Since critics spend most of their time managing "on behalf of the audience" the second-rate literature produced by the existing literary system, few of them have noticed the new movement (to be fair, it's not the critics' fault: it is the pseudo-erudite journalists'; the critics, as we all know, can only notice those things that are sent to them by the press offices of the big publishing houses). When, for instance, at the "Milano-poesia" festival, in 1989, the "Gruppo 93" was born, given the reference to the defunct "Gruppo 63" (which, to tell the truth, is half playful, half parodic, and not surprisingly chosen at the suggestion of the late Corrado Costa, may he rest in peace, during a lunch break at the festival), the reporters concocted (and fed to the audience) the easiest explanation possible: in Italy an avant-garde with two "neos" had just been born.[3] (Bettini and Di Marco, 1993: 8)

The polemic, almost vitriolic tone of these remarks is an integral part of the rhetorical stance adopted by most members of Gruppo 93, as they sought to distance themselves from those writers and critics they considered complicit in a system that encouraged conformity and marginalized all forms of linguistic experimentation.

Corrado Costa, an intellectual and poet who belonged to the neo-avant-garde, a member of the editorial board of the journal *Malebolge*, and thus an important part of Gruppo 63, suggested the new name. The 6 in 63 would be turned upside down, and become a 9. Additionally, and here lies the ironic and parodic dimension of this name, the year 1993 wouldn't mark the inauguration of the movement, but rather its expiration date: at that time everyone would move on to something else (and, in fact, everyone did).

This new attempt to form a poetic avant-garde movement would be the third of the century: the Novecento had already seen Futurism, the neo-avant-garde of Gruppo 63, and now the neo-neo-avant-garde, the third wave mentioned in the title of Bettini and Di Marco's book. Calling it an "avant-garde with two 'neos'" is clearly a way of belittling it, especially if one remembers that "neo" in Italian means "mole:" the face of this new movement was already marked, from birth, by two blemishes, as the Italian saying implies.

The "second-rate literature" that Di Marco finds so intolerable is the product of an increasingly more consolidated publishing industry[4] that pushes for what Gruppo 93 considered an innocuous and mainstream version of postmodernism, while marginalizing any attempt to build a more thoughtful, experimental alternative; only a few of the older poets resisted, following their personal path of research, surrounded by an almost complete indifference.

Here is a long quote from the insightful monograph by Federica Santini, who does an excellent job of summarizing the cultural landscape between the end of the neo-avant-garde (in 1969, with the closing of the journal *Quindici*), and the late 1970s and early 1980s:

> During the years of "contestazione" [the civil unrest spreading in the US and Europe around 1968], literature, the product of the bourgeois world, was seen as inessential, perhaps even a tool for class oppression. The journal *Quindici*, which ceased publication in July 1969, had marked a switch away from writing and toward political action, leaving in all of its participants a sense of shame for being writers, for working on a product of the bourgeois world, rather than being active participants in the political struggle. At the end of the decade, however, this polemic tension began to relax: at the beginning of the 1970s, politics lost its central role within the cultural life of the nation, and thus the stigma connected to writing poetry was lifted, leading to an unexpected explosion of creativity in this field. Therefore, this moment works as a perfect starting point for our analysis, for at this time, as never before in the Novecento, many authors

were forced to reconsider their work and choose an intellectual path that would lead them in a new direction, completely different from the one they had been following prior to "contestazione."[5] (Santini, 1993: 30)

The great period of experimentations that spanned over a decade, from the mid-1950s to the late 1960s, had come to an end when the editorial board of *Quindici* finally splintered beyond any possible reconciliation over the issue of what role literature should play in facilitating the beginning of a social and political revolution. For many intellectuals, writing was not enough anymore: the times called for a direct intervention in the political struggle. Furthermore, the very act of writing had become suspicious and morally questionable: removing oneself from the tumultuous events that were shaking Italy and Europe in order to put pen to paper was seen as a refusal to face the "enemy" directly, an act of intellectual timidity if not outright cowardice. Thus the sense of shame mentioned by Santini.

It is important we make a distinction, here, between an active participation to the political life of the country through protests, marches, strikes, and rallies on the one hand, and a pursuit of political objectives in the public sphere through the manipulation of the linguistic means deployed in one's poetry. While the first kind of political activism was alive and well throughout the 1970s, the second showed the first signs of fatigue and crisis much earlier, half way through the decade. In this sense, Santini is correct in stating that "at the beginning of the 1970s, politics lost its central role within the cultural life of the nation."

Mastropasqua also looks at the first half of that same decade as the point of origin for the long-term historical and cultural processes that would lead to a shift toward the private life and a disengagement from active politics and the public sphere (at least in poetry):

> These are writers, critics, and intellectuals that were working against the tide in a time, the second half of the 1970s, when a phase of restoration and reaction was starting. This new phase was aimed at watering down and squandering all the innovative and traumatic elements introduced into culture and the literary practice by the ethical and political tensions that had culminated in the events of 1968, while bringing back anachronistic values and ideologies, centered around individualism, private life, lyrical effusions, and the exceptional role of poetry. The cultural recession of the 1970s has actually found a fertile ground in the disaggregation of large numbers of leftist intellectuals who were faced with the structural crisis of the first half of the decade. (Mastropasqua, 1993: 74-75)

The poets and intellectuals that Gruppo 93 chose as their adversaries – those who are guilty of "watering down and squandering," as Mastropasqua put it, all the hard-earned innovations introduced by the two previous waves of avant-gardes – are not always clearly identified. They often remain a vague cohort of unnamed foes, so much so that one wonders whether they really exist or, rather, they might just be a rhetorical device, adopted to transform a loose association of writers into an organic "group."[6] Additionally, their poetry is never quoted directly: is it really that reactionary and impervious to the recent experiments? Once more, we can turn to Mastropasqua:

> With the resurgence of neo-capitalism and the unchecked expansion of a global market ideology, the ephemeral and neo-romanticism are absorbed and amplified by the cultural industry, that enhances their intrinsic potential for becoming spectacles and turns them into objects for ready and easy consumption. Good examples of this phenomenon are, on the one hand, the two anthologies *Il pubblico della poesia* (*The public of poetry*) and *La parola innamorata* (*The enamored word*); on the other hand, the contemporaneous festival-like gatherings of Castelporziano and Piazza Siena.[7] (Matropasqua, 1993: 75)

Bettini and Muzzioli, in the foreword to their book dedicated to Gruppo 93, identify these same anthologies as the expression of those undesirable literary trends they were fighting against:

> The targets are the generational trends apparent in the anthologies *Il pubblico della poesia* (The public of poetry, Lerici, 1975) and *La parola innamorata* (The enamored word, Feltrinelli, 1978): these trends would be the first ones to be defined, with a term that would later become very popular, as "neo-romantic poetry." Against their poetics – based on fake inspiration, facile confessions, sudden and intermittent illuminations – *Quaderni* proposes a conflictual hypothesis based, as the formula "materialistic writing" suggests, on clear-cut choices, the material substance of the text, a sense of politics "mediated" by linguistic, pragmatic, and cognitive functions. (Bettini and Muzzioli, 1990: 15)

According to the editors of *Quaderni di critica*, the vast majority of the new poetry that was being published marked a step back toward a more traditional style, that was mostly averse to any linguistic experimentation. To the already mentioned and quite influential *Il pubblico della poesia*, edited by Alfonso Berardinelli and Franco Cordelli, and *La parola innamorata*, edited by Giancarlo Pontiggia and Ezio Di Mauro, we can add *Poesia degli anni Settanta* (Poetry of the 1970s, 1979) edited by Antonio Porta.

Obviously, there are many exceptions to the grim picture painted by Muzzioli, and some of the poetry contained in these volumes would appeal even to the members of Gruppo 93. One example over all others: Maurizio Cucchi. His poetic debut with *Il disperso* (*The Missing*, 1976) was favorably received by the vast majority of writers and *addetti ai lavori*, including the members of Gruppo 93.[8] At the same time, the authors of the previous generation were still quite active, publishing books of consistently high quality (one could mention, for instance, Elio Pagliarani, Edoardo Cacciatore, and Emilio Villa, and the list could go on).

Before moving any further, it is important we provide at least some examples of the theoretical texts produced by the writers that have been so harshly criticized, in order to judge for ourselves whether their depiction is in any way respondent to the truth. We can start with the definition of poetry given by Pontiggia and Di Mauro in the preface to their anthology, entitled "La statua vuota" ("The Empty Statue"):

> Thus, the poetic word is:
> — *enamored*, hence impertinent and sardonic, indifferent to the solemn declarations and conclaves of justice;
> — *colorful*, for it doesn't trace drawings or connections, nor is it the line that goes from truth to error as the recognition of a truth, but rather it creates the burning (and blinding) disorientation of a separation from meaning that is the appearance of that separation, its dissimulation;
> — *enrapturing*, hence it involves a movement of seduction and removal during which the thing is not approached or taken away from sight, but leads to a landscape in which, suddenly, one is caught by that space and the thing turns into something else, into the other, that is the language of the origins. (Pontiggia and Di Mauro, 1978: 11)

The difference in tone, language, and ideological framework between the editors of *La parola innamorata* and Gruppo 93 is immediately clear. The kind of poetry prefigured by Pontiggia and Di Mauro is the polar opposite of the engaged, self-aware, experimental practice which some of the intellectuals of the group dubbed "scrittura materialistica," that is "materialistic writing." In fact, the enamored word is "indifferent to the solemn declarations of justice," and thus, one can extrapolate, it rejects a direct participation in the political life of the country.

The objective of "parola innamorata" is not to reach a sense of truth (not even in the diminished sense of an historically-determined truth), whose existence is strongly doubted, but rather that of prolonging the moment of confusion and indecisiveness, the surprise and the delight of discovery, the very precious feelings that are so rare and so ephemeral in the everyday life of language, but that can be carefully planned in poetry, and then enshrined to stand the test of time, like fragile insects trapped in amber.

In order to achieve this effect, the relationship with the reader must be predicated on artifice: the tools of the craft cannot be exhibited and critiqued (as is routinely the case in "scrittura materialista"), but rather hidden from view, in order to amplify the final impact of the composition. Such a relationship, inevitably, implies an asymmetry between author and audience, as well as a good measure of deception. In fact, right after the passage quoted above, Pontiggia and Di Mauro write "la poesia usa i lettori, non è usata," that is to say "poetry uses readers, it is not used by them;" once again, a stand that is diametrically opposed to the one expressed in many occasions by Muzzioli, Bettini, and the other critics of Gruppo 93.[9]

If this is the relationship with the general audience, how do Pontiggia and Di Mauro envision the one with the specialists of literature? Here is another excerpt from "La statua vuota:"

> Thus we say no to the historicist criticism and its sociologizing ramifications that follow the national line De Sanctis-Gramsci (with contaminations from Croce and Luckacs) and that mandates poetry's tactical approach to history and the social sphere as well as the *entirely* ethical and political mission entrusted to art (positive values, exemplarity, ideological content, reflection, etc.) that finds an archaic and grotesque key stone in the pinnacles of *Quaderni* [*del carcere*], like, for example, "the logical and historical-actual coherence of historically represented masses of sentiments."[10] (Pontiggia and Di Mauro, 1978: 9-10)

Poetry, according to the two editors, is not something that can be explained, taught, approached from a sociological or historical perspective, but rather it is something that must be witnessed and experienced intuitively, at a deep, emotional level. In fact, those who try to explain it, kill it, breaking the spell and spoiling all the fun:

> Hence, those who believe in the opposition between contents, in lived experiences, in "something to be said" and "something to be done," in a subject that is organic to a given time and place, [...] there they are, organizing conferences, poetic "practices," seminars, they want to "understand," "clarify," neutralize the bristly, branchy (and yet always airy) page with the aseptic, mortuary snowflakes of sociology, audiences, churches and homologations, indignations and reassuring verifications [...] while they don't listen to the dance steps, to the fingers of love through which those who launched

the thread, simultaneously, made the Palace disappear, inviting their lover to the joy of a verse that cannot be described. (Pontiggia and Di Mauro, 1978: 16)

The criticism of Gruppo 93 is focused especially on these characteristics of the new trends in poetry, which they see as a form of betrayal of what they considered the ultimate mission of literature and art: to provide the audience with efficient tools to interpret and transform reality. The two approaches (Gruppo 93's on the one hand, and that of some of the new poets that debuted in the 1970s, on the other) couldn't be further apart. In summarizing the difference, the editors of *Quaderni di critica*[11] use the opposition symbol v. allegory: their vision for poetry is allegorical; their adversaries', symbolic. Here is a brief passage from an article entitled "Allegoria e antagonismo" (Allegory and antagonism), included in the already-mentioned volume *Terza Ondata*:

> In regard to the intimistic and escapist poetics that have been the contingent and circumscribed object of our criticism, and which we intend to leave behind, the contraposition between allegory and symbol is of crucial importance and the source of a cultural divide that determines all other, more specific and apparent distinctions in ideological, linguistic, and behavioral matters. The characteristics attacked and stigmatized belong to the evocative area of poetic language. And thus the celebration of the private sphere, the search for what is ineffable, the escape into the myth, the exaltation of poetry as an absolute and privileged value are all dependent on the sphere of symbol and its synchronic updating in an autobiographical and pseudo-mystical version. (Bettini and Di Marco, 1993: 277)

Bettini and his fellow editors connect the "evocative area of poetic language" with a form of escapism that, they believe, reduces poetry to a mere form of entertainment and renounces its socio-political mission. This "symbolic" approach drives the poems away from the current cultural context and into a rarefied "autobiographical and pseudo-mystical" dimension.

Before we move on to analyzing a sample of Bàino's poems, there are a few more distinctions that need to be made; as mentioned above, it would be wrong to imply that Gruppo 93 held a united front in matters of aesthetics and politics: its members entertained different opinions regarding the way in which the experimentation in poetry should proceed, and whether or not a frontal opposition to the much despised neo-romantic and postmodern poets was even possible.

For the sake of brevity and clarity, I will simplify the positions involved by saying that there were two main currents within Gruppo 93: a first, which we will call "frontalisti," advocated a direct opposition to the cultural status quo, believing that it was still possible to organize an avant-garde movement capable of articulating a contradiction to the amorphous postmodern system they were facing. Among the intellectuals in this camp we can include the editors of *Quaderni di ricerca*, and in particular Francesco Muzzioli, Mario Lunetta, Filippo Bettini, and Roberto Di Marco. Here is a quote from an article by Bettini, now collected in the already mentioned volume *Terza Ondata*, that summarizes this group's opinion regarding the possibility of forming an avant-garde movement:

> There are three essential conditions within which the genesis of each cycle of avant-garde movement can be inscribed: the existence of a widespread state of conformism; the unfolding of an "epochal" phase of transition and radical change; the objective need for a different connection between literature, politics, and society. Nowadays all three conditions can be verified in the phenomenology of the juncture in which we find ourselves. (Bettini and Di Marco, 1993: 54)

Bettini and the editors of *Quaderni di ricerca* believed that the formation of avant-garde movements was a cyclical phenomenon that happened whenever certain conditions were fulfilled; in their estimation that was the third time such conditions presented themselves in the Novecento. Therefore, the birth of a new avant-garde was just a matter of coordinating the will of the intellectuals involved: the very discussion they were having was proof that it was still possible to formulate an opposition to postmodernism and the mainstream cultural system.

Many criticized Bettini's position by pointing out that his understanding of how an avant-garde movement was formed and operated was flawed: he was considering the problem from a perspective that was too abstract, and did not account for the more pragmatic aspects that allowed such movements to exist and operate within society. Petrella does an excellent job at summarizing this point:

> In other terms, no answer is provided to the question: "how can we conquer the spaces suitable for divulging and imposing the contradiction, the *shock*, or, at any rate, the products of the avant-garde?" The editors of *Quaderni di ricerca*, as well as many other members of *Gruppo 93* have not addressed this issue. Although they provided a detailed theoretical approach, they failed to elaborate the additional step that would have enabled them to capture the public's imagination and impose their views. [...] the conquest of cultural space cannot be achieved solely through one's message, but must be pursued through constant and sustained extra-textual action. In fact, the objective of every avant-garde is to reach as vast an audience as possible, no matter how problematic this can be in a social and cultural environment such as the postmodern one. (Petrella, 2010:19)

In order for the opposition to the establishment expressed by an avant-garde movement to have any meaning, it has to be present in the public sphere; for its breach with tradition and cultural institutions to carry any political meaning, the actions and writings of its members must be known to as many people as possible. The neo-avant-garde had been successful because it was able to occupy, although briefly, the center of the intellectual life of the country. In the aftermath of its disbandment, the cultural and political system had grown immune to the provocations and the theatrical gestures of the avant-garde. In fact, the cultural industry might even have welcomed a third wave of avant-garde, if only its protagonists had accepted to be "managed," to use Di Marco's expression.

And here is the paradoxical situation in which Gruppo 93 found itself: if its members wanted their message to have an audience, they had to accept a set of conditions (both practical and ideological) that would have diluted it beyond recognition; conversely, if they decided to hold on to their independence, and keep the integrity of their message, the chance of reaching a large enough audience was negligible.

The "frontalisti" were convinced it was still possible to achieve both goals without compromising; a second current, which we will call "lateralisti," did not share their conviction, and advocated for a more oblique strategy to oppose and contradict the status quo. Pietro Cataldi, another important voice in the debate within Gruppo 93, expressed this position very clearly, although he posited it as a commonly shared belief within the group:

> [...] the authors of Gruppo 93 find no longer feasible the very notion of creating an avant-garde movement. In fact, the modus operandi of the avant-garde is historically defined as the aspiration to occupy the center of the cultural space, and the formal rupture it creates is seen as carrying an intrinsic political meaning. Conversely, the various members of Gruppo 93 acknowledge the irreparable corruption of the cultural mechanisms and their relation with the "system" of power; and thus a leaning toward the margins of the cultural system seems a more suitable approach. [...] The experimentation on language and, most of all, through language, is charged with the responsibility, of an ethical rather than political nature, to resist and mount a counterattack. (Cataldi, 1994: 183)

As a response to the cultural and social situation, and to the impasse that threatened to strangle any form of resistance and contradiction, Cataldi suggests a move toward the margins, a lateral shift that would allow intellectuals to exploit the contradictions within the postmodern system and make them work for their neo-avant-garde agenda. Unfortunately, this would lead to the abandonment of any explicit participation in politics: literature, according to Cataldi, was no longer capable of influencing in any meaningful way the political life of the country. Yet, it could still perform a public function by working on an ethical plane, denouncing the moral corruption of the establishment through an experimental use of language; thus, he indicates a direction forward, a way of making literature relevant once more.

Giving up on a direct involvement with politics is not something these writers do lightly: they are fully aware of all the ramifications such a loss entails. The group around the journal *Altri Luoghi* (Marco Berisso, Piero Cademartori, Guido Caserza, Paolo Gentiluomo) speaks of a "letteratura minore" as the result of such a diminished set of aspirations:

> [...] proposing a literature that is devoid of a large-scale plan, a "resistance" kind of literature, that hasn't chosen as its objective the remaking of the world, or the remaking of the world's structures, is inevitably the same as proposing a lesser literature. But it seems to us that "lesser literature" is a label that can be used not only to describe our own work, but perhaps also the entirety of the literary output of the last twenty years [...]. We would also like to state in a similarly unequivocal manner that if literature is not capable of changing the world, neither is it its job to console it. (Berisso et al., 1993: 34)

In addition to all the bitterness for the sacrifice they are asked to make in order to preserve their independence, we can also see the strong resolution of these intellectuals to never act as mere providers of escapist entertainment: if the role of planning a new and better world cannot be performed by literature any longer, they will reluctantly (but effectively) take on a lesser role: cultivating a sense of beauty and engagement with humanity and nature that is alternative and in contradiction to the hedonistic, narcissistic, and consumeristic attitude prominent everywhere else in culture.

Besides the "frontalisti" and "lateralisti," the two currents already described, there is a third group, made up mostly of those authors who did not express a strong preference, and often tried to mediate between the two distinct tendencies within Gruppo 93. As mentioned above, this is an extremely simplistic way of summarizing the positions at play: much more could be said about the debates, the articles, the conferences, and the brilliant exchanges that have grown around these issues. In fact, we could learn a great deal from the resolve shown by some of these authors, and the ingenious devices they have conceived to overcome the impossible situation in which they found themselves. Following this path any further, however, is beyond the scope of this introduction.

Before closing this section, it is important we place Bàino within this larger discussion. He, along with his fellow editors of *Baldus* (Biagio Cepollaro and Lello Voce), belonged to the "lateralisti" faction, but often expressed, on the pages of their journal, a slightly different position, adopting the label of "postmodernisti critici," that is "critical postmodernists." It was their opinion that the solution to the double bind in which Gruppo 93 found itself was to be found in a strategic use of the tools that postmodernism made available to them: through a careful manipulation of traditional and canonical texts, combined with audacious and unscrupulous linguistic experimentations, it was possible to articulate an opposition to what they considered the bland, reactionary status quo and reach, at the same time, a vast audience. Their approach was focused on practice, on the application of allegorical tools to their verse, and, especially in Bàino's case, there was an instinctual mistrust for the excesses of theory, that seemed to have monopolized the discussion. Here is a brief passage from an article by Luperini who, in the first issue of *Baldus*, summarizes the essential traits of its editors' position:

> speaking of critical postmodernism means to restore a communicative rationality – that is a sense of purpose, syntax, allegorism – to a situation that postmodernity has seen in terms of juxtaposition, parataxis, symbolism. It means to make a critical use of contamination. (Luperini, 1991: 30)

The importance assigned to contamination is clearly highlighted, as well as the preference given to allegorism over symbolism.[12] With the term "syntax," Luperini seems to imply a varied and nuanced organization of the text at all levels: prosodic, rhetorical, but also in the treatment of the source materials, taken from the literary tradition as well as popular culture. The first dichotomy, between "juxtaposition" and "sense of purpose," is rather more opaque: he probably had in mind, on the one hand, the way in which the various linguistic elements were put together by these authors (merely juxtaposed, in the case of postmodernism; melded, mixed, and staggered, with the intention of creating a specific effect or meaning, in the case of critical postmodernism). On the other hand, he might have been thinking of the greater political issues we have been discussing: while the "lateralisti" were attempting a maneuver intended to beat the mainstream culture at its own game, the "frontalisti" were looking to achieve their goal through a direct confrontation, "juxtaposing" their system of values with that of the establishment.

As mentioned by Luperini, the three poets of *Baldus* share an allegorical approach to literature; at the textual level, such an approach takes the form of two complementary strategies: *citazionismo*, that is "citationism," and multilinguism. Here is how Petrella defines these terms:

> Contamination is essentially achieved when one joins (in a dialogic and non-mimetic way) two distinct units forming a third entity that is not a synthesis but rather a hybrid. This new text will not conflate the two linguistic codes, but will embrace intertextuality as an expression of the complexity of reality. Therefore, contamination becomes one of the main expressions of allegorism, and can draw upon numerous literary techniques. First among them is citation, as theorized by Benjamin: a way of ripping a fragment from the indistinct historical *continuum* in order to invest it with new meaning, or to save it from the oblivion in which the official tradition has exiled it. Thus, citazionismo can be practiced as the sematic plagiarism of a canonical author or as the rediscovery of a literary canon that exists beyond any form of conformism. (Petrella. 2010: 22)

Often Bàino and the other poets of *Baldus* appropriate the least solemn passages from lesser known texts by canonical authors, weaving together a subtle and complex network of allusions and echoes that lends a sense of obscurity and impenetrability to their poetic creations while, at the very same time, lowering and almost ridiculing the sources from where they derive their materials. They build an endless chain of signification that strings together several signs, all internal to literature, in an ever-shifting fugue of references. Yet – and here lies the allegorical dimension of this textual strategy – this entire edifice of quotations is a way of pointing to the real world that exists outside of literature, it is a last-ditch effort to somehow implicate reality through the elusive rhetorical means that are still available to the author.

An excellent example of this allegorical, ironic use of a canonical text can be seen in the following passage, taken from the second half of Bàino's *Fax giallo* (*Yellow fax*, 1993):

> (umbrella di mendicante, giostra fosforescente di cavalluzzi
> marini), come t'intana la primavera metallizzata dei coralli,
> il mucchio d'ostriche (cofano di sputi e perle), quanto si
> latita tra l'oloturie (di cenciaiuolo verminosi sacchi),
> dietro l'attinia (insanguinato ceppo ove lasciarono capelli
> serpini sirene decapitate), in mezzo ai verdi vermi
> delle alghe, dietro quel cassettone o nella stanza di là,
> sotto il letto dichiscrissedimare la balfigola diosalvi
> dalpalombaroboiasottomarinoacrobataprofondoburattino
> nelteatromutodeipescispauracchiobecchinomascheratuomopneumatico
> che aiuta con l'arpione l'infinito ad essere... il cruento
> cugino mare... dal fax affiora fievole la nota di una diaspora[13] (Bàino, 1993a)

The whole passage is based on a series of quotations from the text included in the famous visual poem by Corrado Govoni, entitled "Il Palombaro" ("The Deep-Sea Diver").[14] All the elements of this rather unusual underwater scene (jellyfish, seahorses, oysters, corals, sea cucumbers, anemones, seaweed) as well as all the terms of comparison used to describe them (beggar's umbrella, merry-go-round, chest, sack, bloody trunk, serpent hair) are taken from that source, but they appear shuffled, re-glued together, and are rendered almost unrecognizable. The sense of eerie stillness already present in the original is thus strangely amplified. A similar reorganization is performed on another classic, only this time it is one of those poems so famous, so universally known, that it can withstand a much more violent intervention:

> la pampa fondocupa dell'udito): c'è chi s'allamana d'ammansa
> s'ellemene d'emmense d'imminsi s'illimini s'ollomono
> d'ommonso d'ummunsu s'ullumunu col core in rogo di chi crede[15] (Bàino, 1993a)

This is the second stanza of *Fax giallo*, and the source text is clearly Ungaretti's "Mattina."[16] The brevity of the poem allows Bàino to reiterate it five times, each time substituting all the vowels for just one. Perhaps, after being recited by generations of school children, the only thing that remains of this beautiful poem, written by one of the great masters of the Twentieth Century, is just a soundscape, a string of consonants and vowels that Bàino attempts to revitalize through a game of permutation. Or, maybe, he intends to call attention to the paradoxes of fame, and its influence on the relationship with the readers; or, finally, it is a pessimistic pronouncement on all poetry: no matter how powerful and sophisticated, it can be instantly emptied and rendered useless. In fact, it might very well be that the sense of this quote is a combination of the three possibilities we just offered, for all three can find a place and a justification in the multi-layered universe woven together by Bàino.

His allusion to Rimbaud's poem "Vowels," included at the very end of *Fax giallo*, confirms the importance of what, at first sight, could appear as just a light-hearted game. Here is the passage:

> vostraloro pazzeria (del tipo inventa il vocalico dei colori
> : nero Aico, bianco Eico, rosso Iico, blu Oico, verde Uico),[17] (Bàino, 1993a)

The relationship that Rimbaud had established between vowels and colors is inverted. According to the French poet, the vowel "a" is black, while "e" is white, "I" red, and so on. Bàino, instead, decides to upend the hierarchy between language and the world: the color black is "aicous," that is, it has a quality that reminds one of the vowel "a;" the color white is "eicous," and so on.

As it is clear even from just the verses quoted so far, another important trait of this poetry is multilinguism. To the different varieties of Italian, ranging from the archaic and literary to the contemporary and demotic, one must add French, Spanish, a great many neologisms, and a significant injection of dialect. As mentioned by Petrella, this wide variety of codes is not simply mixed or juxtaposed; it is melded together and made into a hybrid, a completely new linguistic creation that, while bearing some of the characteristics of the different parts that compose it, behaves in radically different ways. Here is a quote from an article by Antonio Paghi, published in *Baldus*:

> The lexicon unites Italian and dialect, foreign languages and terms taken from literary idiolects, bits of jargon and specialized codes, low-brow words (sometimes openly trivial ones) and high-brow ones (often hyper-educated). Equally important is the formation of "strong" neologisms, the result of two separate writing techniques that frequently end up overlapping. The first exploits the torsion (the spastic spasm, as Gadda would put it) that Bàino imposes upon the linguistic objects [...]. The second involves the peculiar creation of "hybrid and creolingual children" based on the disassembly and reassembly (in a critical and contaminated way) of the different elements of the same linguistic corpus, charged with an ironic and expressive energy [...]. But it is on the axis of syntagmatic combination that this idiolect reaches its full potential, utilizing a wide lexical array within a systematic juxtaposition of terms taken from very distant, sometimes opposite areas. (Paghi, 1994: 67)

Paghi does an excellent job of listing the different components that make up Bàino's experimental code; particularly interesting is his idea that there are two main techniques through which neologisms are built. The first one, he argues, recalls Gadda's expressionism: a force that reshapes language from the inside out, twisting and deforming it in an attempt to make it fit the ever-shifting reality that exists outside of it. Here is a small example:

> capitoli indici d'argomenti... el siglo siécolo che schiuppa
>   millenario (millénaire qui meurt...) scaca suoi semi sue sfa
> ccimme da fior festaiolo: patullano parole   papareggiano (da pa
>   perepapesse): in broda universale agguazzano aggallan musiche
>   mappe immagini dati&archivi virtualmente e senza fine l'i
>   pertesto... (dal fax tafàni diafani scribillano scrivòlano: alla
>   Volvo di Uddevalla lo vogliono devoto dell'azienda l'operaio)...[18]
> (Bàino, 1993a)

We can see many of the different idioms employed by Bàino, and how he modifies, distorts, and re-shapes them to fit the reality he is trying to describe. In addition to standard Italian, we encounter Spanish, French, Neapolitan, as well as an in inordinate amount of neologisms: "patullano," "papareggiano," "agguazzano" all express the same idea of something floating over water; "scribillano" and "scrivòlano" are innovative versions of the verb "to write," or "scrivere."

The second technique described by Paghi is more macaronic in nature, and aims at modifying the linguistic code by positioning the speaker on the outside, in the interstitial space that divides two different languages: the gaps between Italian and French, Italian and Spanish, Italian and different dialects become the fertile spaces from which "hybrid and creolingual children"[19] may spring forth. Words are disassembled, reduced to their smallest components, often re-invented according to fantastical etymologies, and then reassembled in a completely different context, adopting the morphology of a new idiom. Here are two of the most representative instances in *Fax giallo*; the first mocks the language of technology, hybridizing English and Italian to form a series of new words:

> ha interfacce del dopo del dopo Silicon Valley in gommaresina
>   di facce ha interfacce di organo nuovo del dopo le schede
> ed i mouse videare calzante si adatta in procelle di pelle
> [...]
>   da attila la vecchia tecnica dotta?... outputta il fax, gra
> ffia prefetti offrendo i fatti di una nera pantera d'una jatta[20] (Bàino, 1993a)

The second example uses French as the basis for a different kind of macaronic idiom:

> nontiscordardimé, di gialla luce con sua ombra viola (en fransé
>   mozzarellà: magàr non è toute une boutanade il dir que il gran
>   problem è plus la relation col mond que le mystère du mond),
> lector, e st'alkimia del dire è storia di una miatuasuanostra[21] (Bàino, 1993a)

One cannot help but feel Emilio Villa's strong influence on these verses (and, in particular, that of his *Heurarium*).[22] In this case, however, Bàino's intention seems to be more playful, as he deploys Villa's linguistic tools and mixes them with the portentous tongue devised by Totò and Peppino in that famous scene with the Milanese street cop in *Totò, Peppino e la malafemmina* (1956).

Going back to Paghi's article, his last observation is equally insightful, for it points out how the same techniques of hybridization are practiced also at the syntagmatic level, in the way the different elements of the poem are put together: the interaction between different words; the radical re-arranging of quotations, broken up and rebuilt in ways that don't take into account the original context; and, finally, the parsing of different lines, which often relies on strong enjambments that cut through individual words, splitting them in two halves (and examples of these techniques can be seen in the verses quoted so far). All the empty space that is thus cleared (between words, quotations, and lines) is rendered available to the reader, who is invited to participate in the creation of the work by activating its process of signification. The poem opens up onto the world just when its textual strategies seem to push it further away from the plain speech of everyday people.

However, the most interesting aspect of this book is, perhaps, its reflection on technology and its effects on identity, self, and authorship. This issue resonates with many writers of Gruppo 93, and is a common preoccupation in the Italian culture at the end of last century. Here is a brief quote from Petrella that summarizes these concerns:

> The dominance of mass media transforms Western society into a mediatic universe, whose life is ruled by images and instantaneous communication: the new technologies and the acceleration of our life styles, as philosopher Paul Virilio argues in his *Aesthetics of Disappearence*, imply not only a distortion of perception but also a loss of historical memory. [...] History and its epochs disappear, leaving behind a space that is undivided, instantaneous, immediate and freely accessible. (Petrella, 2010: 89)

The disappearance of history allows Bàino's contaminations to bring together materials from the most disparate historical and geographical origins, creating striking poetic hybrids. A wonderful emblem of this media environment and its effects on language, something of a real-life mythological beast, is the wholphin, that Bàino translates as "balfino" including it among the many underwater creatures that populate his *Fax giallo*:

>   [...] informa
> il fax d'un bel balfino nato in vascacquatile di Kioto o To
>   kio: avrà più dei 2 metri e 9 di papà delfino, ché maman
> balena è lunga cinque (e scorcia pinne e zinne ad usum, come dir?,
>   Balphini): e che tu vada a spigole, se vuoi, in tirrene
>   mucillagini: la balfigola prole in lunghi corridoi di sottomare

> si districhi e diporti, illesa fra i silenti monnezzai profondi,
> il cellulòideo occhio ponderante quanto scherma la medusa[23] (Bàino, 1993a)

What would appear as yet another one of the poet's creations, one of his "hybrid and creolingual children," is an actual animal (the offspring of a female common bottlenose dolphin and a male false killer whale), first bred in captivity at Tokyo's SeaWorld in 1981.[24] This fascinating bit of trivia is closely followed, in the next stanza, by the quotation/reinterpretation of Govoni's "Deep-sea diver," which we have already discussed. It doesn't matter, Bàino seems to imply here, where the verbal materials come from, they could a real news item or the fantasy of a writer long-dead: everything can be combined, dismantled and reassembled in the inexorable unfolding of his "fax."

Not only is reality transmuted into a perennial flux of accelerated and potentially interchangeable particles, identity itself becomes a field of possibilities rather than a concrete and coherent entity. Here is another, rather long, quote from an article by Gian Paolo Renello:

> In *Fax giallo* [...] the catalyst for the composition is a medium of communication, by now widely used, that presents a new characteristic when compared to previous mass media (and to the telephone): it does not communicate orally, and it does so anonymously. The text seems to be mimicking this new tool's mode of operation. The various communicative fluxes can, theoretically, be arriving from any given part of a space that is essentially undetermined, perhaps even without anyone on the receiving end [...]. The metaphor of the fax allows Bàino a great freedom to choose his materials, by using the fiction of the medium's anonymity and its independence from the sources. In reality, this operation leads to two different modes of action: he can reproduce and rearrange, sometimes in a fragmentary fashion, shards of conversations that have not necessarily been transmitted via fax, and mix them together; alternatively, and this is the most interesting aspect, he can interface a personal, multilevel reality with a new communicative system. Memory and thought can pour through the connection of words and onto the page in an almost torrential, unstoppable way, to the point that the connection itself is obstructed, rendered almost impassable. Thus we see fluxes of words that are almost uninterrupted, completely indistinguishable at first sight, since they are not graphically separated; their reading and their pronunciation requires a visual exercise and a true breathing *performance* that is almost impossible. In this phase, where words are compressed one on top of the other, bound and separated to form new terms, the poem becomes an explosion of a technological and archaic psyche. (Renello, 1993: 32)

Bàino does not usually write explicitly about his poems and his poetics. Here below is a rare exception: a letter he sent to Francesco Muzzioli regarding his

Fax giallo, dated October 2000, that he was kind enough to share with me. It contains some invaluable insights regarding his verses:

> *Fax giallo*, for me, is a way of reflecting on the radical changes, the disconnections of the world (symbolized, at a certain point of the text, by the storm, but more on this later). [...] "The idea of the fax that is constantly interrupting the stream of consciousness [...] reflects the need to point at the violent pressure exercised on the contemporary subject by the technologies and the *mass of imagery* that interfere with the I, upset it, thwart its attempts to establish itself as a center." In connection to these issues, [I] tried to accept the challenge that the post-modern condition poses to all writers, forcing them to choose the communicative modes of the *pastiche*. In my text [...] the theme of rain, the *déluge* (the storm I mentioned above), is expressed through a *pastiche* that uses both a "primary text" (*Rain in the Pine Grove*, by D'Annunzio), and a "secondary text," which is its parody (*It's Raining*, by Montale). It was an attempt to bring within the *pastiche*, the *appropriate* expressive form for the postmodern era (provided that is the case; but that is Jameson's hypothesis, which I have embraced, along with the other members of Gruppo '93), some critical and unpredictable elements.[25]

It is remarkable how parody, a tool so commonly used by Bàino in his poems, is here elevated to the second power, in an effort to problematize its deployment within the poetic text: a testament to the critical self-awareness of these verses. Here is the passage in question:

> tout un univers de villes auriculaires... odi? la pioggia cade
>   su la solitaria verdura con un crepitìo che dura e varia
>   nell'aria secondo le fronde più rade, men rade... piove...
> sul nulla che si fa in queste ore di sciopero generale... piove
>
> sulla cartella esattoriale... ascolta, ascolta... l'accordo delle
>   aeree cicale a poco a poco più sordo si fa sotto il pianto
>   che cresce... piove... sulla greppia nazionale... un canto vi si
>   mesce più roco che di laggiù sale... ascolta... piove...
>   sulla Gazzetta Ufficiale, piove su via Solferino, e il pino
> ha un suono, e il Parlamento altro suono: dal ciel cinerino piove
>   sull'assenza universale che il pianto australe rinfresca: chi
>   sa dove, chi sa dove! Qui piove di nuovo su Ermione, ma ora
>   da Erminia si bagna (col suo vero nome)...[26] (Bàino, 1993a)

Later on, in the same letter, Bàino notes that "in *Fax giallo* is also included, with a little irony, the theme of *virtuality*." This is a precious indication that can alert us to a number of references to the cyberpunk sci-fi genre, scattered throughout the book. In particular, there is a cluster of terms ("microchip," "ciberpiastre," "reti g," "kinomodulo," "Gothick," "Kasual") in the very first stanza of the *poemetto*, that are taken directly from William Gibson's novel, *Count Zero*, which was first published in English 1986, and then translated into Italian as *Giù nel cyberspazio*, in 1990. The progressive de-materialization (or "ant-ification")[27] of the subject, the systematic confusion between elements and materials deriving from various historical and geographical origins, multilinguism, and a pervasive contamination between natural and artificial, organic and inorganic are all key characteristics of this literary genre and of Gibson's novels in particular; therefore, it is not so surprising to find them directly quoted in Bàino's verses.

Finally, it is particularly interesting that the poet chose the fax as the means of communication to symbolize all the themes just listed. His booklet came out in 1993. That same year NCSA Mosaic, the first internet browser, was released, and the world wide web was finally available for commercial and private use. There is a lesson, here, about the obsolescence of technologies that we think immanent, and the endurance of ideas that we think fleeting.

Ônne 'e terra (1994), in spite of being published the year after *Fax giallo*, is a radically different book. It continues many of the experimentations begun in that collection, but imposes a new direction to the research, directing it toward a different object. Before we go any further, here is an early (1995) and detailed review published by Pietro Sarzana in *Studi Novecenteschi*:

> Underneath the deceptively easy division into three parts that structures the book (but the three sections are uneven in terms of length and typology), *Ônne 'e terra* hides a complex, labyrinthic structure, difficult to decipher, that must be analyzed with great care. The first section encompasses eleven fragments labelled in Neapolitan as *Vrénzole* (that is "nugae," to use Catullus' words, or texts of little value); the second is made up of the rich and extensive poemetto *'O ggeniuslò*, the piece de resistance, the center of gravity for this entire system; the third contains nine translations in Neapolitan: three from the Spanish Gòngora, three from the French Frénaud, three from the Italian Sereni. Here, too, we can detect a strong internal disparity of time and culture, further evidence of Bàino's strong predilection for contamination. (Sarzana, 1995: 247)

The composition of the language employed changes: the hybrids are no longer based on standard Italian, but begin with Neapolitan dialect.

> In fact, in *Ônne 'e terra*, as Martignoni points out in her preface, his dialect "is not [...] just another one of the multiple factors at play, but rather the main vehicle, the basic structure, that gathers, manipulates, and modulates the other factors." (Sarzana. 1995: 253)

In much the same way, Marcello Carlino and Aldo Mastropasqua, focus on Bàino's dialect as the most remarkable characteristic of *'O ggeniuslò*:

> [This is a] poemetto in two parts, although the curtain never falls nor rises completely: in the first half, as if in the "elsewhere" of a facing translation, the city and the crowd – the former necessary to the latter, in spite of it being monstruous, tentacular – are the head and tail of a snake that forms, uniting its extremities, a circle. The only problem is that the second circle doesn't close: between the complete comformity of the crowd and the rot that plagues and erodes the city [...], the *genius loci*, understood as a point of intersection and the fertile ground for a possible identity [...], is left suspended with a question mark. In the meanwhile, the dialect that declares *apertis verbis* its plurilinguistic inclinations, dialoguing with the French and the Italian, is charged with the task of reflecting and researching, that is of questioning, while the added value of theatricality positions the text in a place (the "geniuslò" of this kind of writing) of estrangement. (Carlino and Mastropasqua, 1993:106)

If *Fax giallo* looked at the progressive de-materialization of the "I," *Ônne 'e terra* turns to the city, investigating it through a boldly expressionistic perspective, as if through an altered state of linguistic consciousness.

> As mentioned above, the second half is made up of a large text that, although divided in different fragments, can be considered a unit; it is dedicated to Naples' *genius loci*, a city that is x-rayed and reinterpreted in a visionary manner in all of its contradictions: tentacular and multi-faceted, dejected and picture-perfect, edulcorated and wretched. The structure of the "poemetto" is extremely intricate, and it communicates a feeling of intense estrangement, for it is parsed by four alphabetic indexes (A, B, a, b): which would lead one to postulate, at least at first, a series of stable distinctions, a sort of "chapters" clearly delineated. But the division in four, which alternates the four indexes, is actually deployed as a highly unstable textual system, whose only discernible trait is "the pulsating impression (deliberately ambiguous) of two distinct rhythms that alternate unpredictably" (C. Martignoni). Thus, this very structure, in all its deceptiveness, seems to almost institute a vertiginous and fractured poetic monologue, that leaves no room for replies and is propelled by the exasperated cry or accusation of contemporary man, who is hopelessly trying to save himself from the ominous decay of the modern metropolis and civilization. (Sarzana, 1995: 248)

One last quote, by this same article, that identifies some of the source materials for Bàino's *poemetto*:

> We can begin, for instance – following the strong theme of the "city" that runs throughout this poetic text dedicated to "all cities" (both Naples and others) – from the central quote that, bitterly but also ironically, brings onstage Baudelaire's lost Paris ("Le vieux Paris n'est plus..."), and retraces the evocation of Zenobia, the "invisible city"

dreamed by Calvino's subtle fantasy, a city that "gives shape to desires" and "where desires either succeed in erasing the city, or are erased by it." Like Zenobia, Naples cannot be catalogued neither among the happy cities nor among the unhappy ones; most importantly, it is a city on the verge of non-being, a city on the brink of sinking forever into the space of memory, the recollection of which can be made permanent by the poet only if its real and life-like characteristics are lost, replaced by his imagination. (Sarzana, 1995: 250)

I would like to add to this brief anthology of the criticism on Bàino's poetry a few more quotations regarding his *Pinocchio (moviole)*, that is *Pinocchio (replays)*, published in 2000. For a quick introduction to this text, we can turn to a contemporary review by Giancarlo Alfano, published in *Il Mattino*:

"pinocchio fleeing/ at dawn, with a nail-like/ rising of the legs." These are the first three verses of Mariano Bàino's *Pinocchio (replays)*, which has been recently published by Piero Manni in Lecce: it is a stunning beginning, that provides a snap-shot of the famous puppet, stuck between an undefinable artificial dimension and the predicaments of a teenager eager to escape the oppressing prospect of facing the adult world. In fact, this is one of the most interesting aspects of Bàino's new book, for the poet has elected to re-tell Collodi's story, but not starting with the transfer of "the piece of wood" from Master Ciliegia's hands to those of Geppetto, nor from the transformation of the inert log into a lively puppet, but rather from Pinocchio's flight from the Law, with his precipitous escape from home and the "father." (Alfano, 2000)

The many interpolations and references added by Bàino to the original story contribute to highlight its more adventurous and rebellious aspects, and bring it closer to the poet's style and sensibility. Here is another passage of that same review:

It's not only a matter of montage, since the Neapolitan poet contaminates his re-writing of Collodi with quotations and allusions to *Hamlet*, Manzoni, *Tristram Shandy*, and also to Shakespeare's *Tempest* (mediated by Eliot's *Waste Land* and, perhaps, Montale's *Mottetti*), Coleridge, and finally *Pinocchio: a parallel book* (1977), by Manganelli. (Alfano, 2000)

As we can see, some of the classics of modern literature are here well represented, as well as some writers whose influence we can easily recognize within the other two chapbooks mentioned above. Consistent is also Bàino's interest for multilinguism; here is a quote from a brief text by Muzzioli, taken from a brochure that summarizes the motivation for the Premio Feronia, awarded to *Pinocchio (moviole)* in 2001:

> Bàino's is a multilingual *Pinocchio*, not only because it has been re-read "from a Neapolitan perspective" (we know its author to be one of the most interesting and lively representatives of the research poetry in Naples), but also because it is approached through a linguistic impasto that brings together spoken dialect, erudite terms, verbal inventions, word play (from "cocomero" [watermelon], for instance, comes "cocco omerico" [Homeric coconut]) and – the author's favourite – macaronic manipulations inspired by the kind of Spanish spoken by a destitute hidalgo, fit for a "low key" ceremony, appropriate to this parodic re-write. There is also a real sense of theatricality: it is not by chance that the episode that remains closest to the original text is the one involving Mangiafuoco, where all the different characters speak directly, as if playing a "central role" and striking their most "dramatic" pose.[28]

Very useful are also Muzzioli's observations regarding the different kinds of verses Bàino has chosen to include:

> The same unstable length that, in the original, characterized the nose of the protagonist, is here applied to the verses, that oscillate both in extension and pace. There are at least three different types: a writing in short stanzas, laid horizontally on the page; a long writing with pauses (marked by curious empty parenthesis, that correspond to as many silences) laid vertically on the page, which usually express a kind of counterpoint; a prose in a smaller font that contains a sort of commentary – the meta-narrative – in which the author mocks himself, an "occasional neo-Collodi," who leaves behind unfinished pieces and "reckless" notes, and finally decides to "resign" from the job taking an ironic step back, abandoning the narrator and objectivizing him into a third person (but then, who is writing? The paradoxes of writing…).[29]

And here is a final consideration regarding the "moviole," the strange subtitle that Bàino adds to his *Pinocchio*:

> The "replays" that Bàino inserted in parethesis next to the name of the archetype he has re-written, are meant as reminders that the ruling principle here is the montage. Montage, a "strong" legacy from the Novecento, is in charge of the game of superimpositions, shifts, clashes, and mixtures of this hyper-literature gone crazy. Through the game of moving from one piece to the next, we can detect something that speaks directly to us: what the text points to, allegorically, is the "warped piece of wood that we are."[30]

As this long introduction draws to its conclusion, I would like to think we have laid out enough proof to show that the poetry of Mariano Bàino and his fellow members of Gruppo 93 deserves many more readers than those it can currently count on. The translations here collected are just a first, imperfect step, but I hope they will encourage students and critics to seek out these authors and their works: many useful, timely strategies can be learned from their study.

Notes

[1] A previous incarnation of this introduction was published as "What's Left of 1963: Mariano Bàino and the Avant-garde with Two 'Nei'" in *Forum Italicum*, 52, n.1, Spring 2018, pp. 153-180.

[2] While, in this volume, we include *Fax giallo* (*Yellow Fax*) in its entirety, we only translated the poemetto '*O Ggeniuslò* from *Ônne 'e terra* and a small selection of texts from *Pinocchio (replays)*.

[3] All translations are mine, unless otherwise noted.

[4] On this issue, see also Schiffrin, 2000.

[5] The periodization offered here by Santini is somewhat controversial. We will discuss it more in detail below.

[6] The resentment toward what they considered a mainstream literature that returned to an outdated aesthetic and invaded all available cultural spaces within the national landscape was one of the main reasons (if not the single greatest reason) that brought together the disparate intellectuals who decided to ban together and form Gruppo 93. These critics and writers often held rather different views of poetry, its social, political, and aesthetic goals, and the tools that were best suited to achieve them, but they all shared a profound dislike for what they saw as an unnecessary step back in matters of poetics. Here is again Muzzioli's assessment of the situation: "[...] the Italian literary scene appears to be marred by a degrading and massive phenomenon, the "return to order." We are in 1981, and for a decade we have been suffering the effects of the nostalgic and traditionalist tendencies that followed the "end of the avant-garde." The best-known players have turned back to a trivial, mannerist, and escapist kind of literature: there has been a return to linear, well laid-out narratives for the novel, and to a revamping of the most antiquated forms of hermetic and post-symbolistic lyricism in poetry. [...] the best part of our literary output has been completely excluded from the official image of the culture of the 1970s, while the second-rate part – that is, the most obsolete, lazy, and tautological part – has taken over, trumping everything else" (Bettini and Muzzioli, 1990: 13). It is also worth pointing out that in this passage Muzzioli agrees with the other writers quoted above when he identifies the beginning of the 1970s as the starting point of that process of progressive disengagement from the political sphere (at least in poetry) and return to a more private dimension.

[7] The poetry festivals mentioned in the quote are the Primo Festival Internazionale di Poesia, held on June 28-30 1979, at Castelporziano, just outside of Rome, near Ostia, and the Festival di poesia, held in Piazza Siena inside the park of Villa Borghese, in Rome, during the summer of 1980.

[8] It is worth mentioning that *La parola innamorata* anthologizes poems from *Il disperso* ("Figure Femminili," "Levataccia," "Nuove ragioni," "Coincidenze"), as well as poems that would be later included in *Le meraviglie dell'acqua*.

[9] See, for instance, Bettini's essay, "Rilivevi oppositivi e proposizioni programmatiche: dalla letteratura del «riflusso» alla nuova letteratura degli anni Ottanta," in Bettini and Muzzioli, 1990: 25-28; "And we will add that the hypothesis of a «materialistic writing», seen from a militant and operative perspective, intends to intervene in the cultural and literary situation [...] claiming for itself and promoting [...] a public and cultural profile that is inspired by an imperative for intransigence, for determination, for a deliberate partisanship, for dialectic openness, for undisguised honesty."

[10] The quotation in this passage is taken from a page of Gramsci's *Quaderni del carcere* in which he praises the kind of politically engaged criticism practiced by De Sanctis; see Gramsci A. (1966) *Letteratura e vita nazionale*, Torino: Einaudi, p. 5. "Dunque no alla critica storicista e alle sue diramazioni sociologizzanti, secondo la linea nazionale De Sanctis-Gramsci (con contaminazioni

ora crociane, ora luckacsiane) che istituisce un avvicinamento tattico della poesia alla storia e al sociale e quella missione *internamente* etica e politica dell'arte (valori positivi, esemplarità, contenuto ideologico, rispecchiamento, ecc.) che trova arcaici e grotteschi archi di volta nei pinnacoli dei *Quaderni* come 'la coerenza logica e storico-attuale delle masse di sentimenti rappresentate storicamente.'"

[11] The article we are about to quote is signed by Filippo Bettini, Marcello Carlino, Aldo Mastropasqua, Francesco Muzzioli, and Giorgio Patrizi.

[12] As already mentioned, the distinction between symbol and allegory is central to the debates of the time. For more details, see the articles collected in the previously quoted *Terza Ondata*... (Bettini and Di Marco, 1993) and *Gruppo '93*... (Bettini and Muzzioli, 1990).

[13] The volume has no page numbers. For the reader's convenience, we copy here our English translation: "(beggar's ombrella, phosphorescent merry-go-round of sea / horsies), how it dens you the metallic spring of corals, / the pile of oysters (trunk of spit and pearls), when someone's / wanted among sea cucumbers (worm-ridden sacks of rag-and-bone man), / behind sea anemones (bloody trunk where decapitated sirens / left their serpent hair), amid the green worms / of seaweed, behind that chest or in that room over there, / under the bed ofthosewhowroteofthesea whalphigolous godsaveus / fromthedeepdiverunderwaterexecutionerdeepacrobatmarionette / inthesilenttheateroffishboogiemanundertakermaskedpneumaticman / who helps the infinite harpoon to be... the gory / sea cousin... from the fax dimly surfaces the note of a diaspora."

[14] Govoni C. (1915) *Rarefazioni e Parole in libertà*. Milano: Edizioni futuriste di "Poesia".

[15] "the bottomdark pampas of the hearing): ammansata anlaghtans some / emmensete enleghtens inlightins immimsiti ommonsoto / onloghtons ummunsutu unlughtuns with the heart on the stake of those who believe."

[16] Ungaretti G. (1919) *Allegria di naufragi*. Firenze: Vallecchi.

[17] Bàino, 1993a. "yourtheir craziness (of the sort invented by the colors' vocalist / : black Aicous, white Eicous, red Iicous, blue Oicous, green Uicous),".

[18] "chapters tables of contents... el siglo siécolo that kicks the bucket / millenary (millénaire qui meurt) dumps his seeds his / cum of festive flower: they ridicule words wallowing (like po / pishducks): in a universal broth splash float music / maps images data&archives virtually and without end the hy / pertext... (from the fax scribrilliant diaphanous gnats slide: at / Volvo in Uddevalla the worker they want him devoted to the company)...".

[19] The expression is Bàino's and is taken from the poem *Quatre-vingt-treize*, first published in Ottonieri, 1992; then it appeared, with minor modifications, in D'Oria, 1993; finally, it was also included in issue 3-4 of *Baldus*, 1994.

[20] "has interfaces of the after of the after Silicon Valley in gum resin / of faces has interfaces of a new organ of the after the discs / and the mice videoing tight adapts into tempests of skin / [...] / like attila the old erudite technique?... the fax outputs, scra / tches prefect offering the fax of a black panther of a kitty."

[21] "of forgetmenots, of yellow light with its purple shade (on fronsay / mozzarellà: maybè its not toot une bullshìt il dir that il grand / problème is plus la relation with the mond than le mystère du mond), / lector, and this alkemy of speech is the history of a myyourhisherour."

[22] Villa E. (1961) *Heurarium*. Roma: Edizioni EX. Villa was also a frequent contributor to the journal *Baldus* for which, as we mentioned, Bàino served as an editor.

[23] "[...] the fax / informs about a nice wholphin born in a waterytank in Kyoto or To / kyo: will

be more than 2 meters long and 9 longer than father dolphin, for maman / whale is five meters long (and cut fins and tits ad usum, shall we say? / Wholphini): and may you fish for seabass, if you want, amid Tyrrhenian / mucilage: may the wholphigolous offspring disentangle and sail through long / underwater corridors, unscathed through silent deep dumpsters, / the celluloid-like eye pondering what the jellyfish hides."

[24] Both the *L.A. Times* and the *Chicago Tribune* published short articles on the wholphin, on the occasion of the birth of the second and third specimens in captivity. They are available at these addresses: http://articles.latimes.com/1987-09-13/news/mn-7448_1_false-killer-whale ; and http://articles.chicagotribune.com/1986-05-18/travel/8602060063_1_wholphin-false-killer-whale-bottlenose.

[25] Mariano Bàino, letter to Francesco Muzzioli, dated "October 2000," provided by the author. "*Fax giallo* è per me una forma d'interrogazione sugli stravolgimenti, sulle sconnessioni del mondo (emblematizzati, in un certo punto del testo, attraverso il tema delle *intemperie*, sul quale tornerò più avanti) [...] "L'idea del fax che di continuo irrompe nel flusso di coscienza [...] risponde alla necessità di alludere alla violenta pressione sul soggetto contemporaneo di tecnologie e di *masse d'immaginario* che interferiscono con l'io, lo sconcertano, ne insidiano i tentativi di costituirsi come centro". In connessione con queste problematiche, [ho] tentato di accettare la sfida che la condizione post-moderna sembra lanciare a chi scrive, obbligandolo alle modalità comunicative del *pastiche*. Nel testo [...], il tema della pioggia e del *déluge* (le intemperie di cui parlavo all'inizio), è espresso nella forma del *pastiche* utilizzando sia un 'testo primo' (*La pioggia nel pineto* di D'Annunzio), sia un 'testo secondo', che ne è la parodia (*Piove*, di Montale). Il tentativo è di portare all'interno del *pastiche*, forma espressiva *propria* dell'era postmoderna (ammesso che sia così; ma tale è l'ipotesi di Jameson, che ho accolto insieme ad altri nel gruppo '93), elementi di criticità e di imprevedibilità."

[26] "tout un univers de villes auriculaires... hear it? the rain falls / on the solitary produce with a crackling that lasts and varies / in the air according to the foliage, thick or thin... it rains... / on the nothing that gets done in these hours of general strike... it rains // on the tax form... listen, listen... the harmony of the / ethereal cicadas little by little dampens and the mounting / cry comes forth... it rains... on the national manger... a coarser / song mixed with it rising from the bottom... listen... it rains... / on the Official Gazette, it rains on via Solferino, and the pine / has one sound, and the Parliament another: from the ashy sky it rains / on the universal absence that the austral cry refreshes: who knows / where, who knows where! Here it rains again on Ermione, but now / at Erminia's she gets wet (under her real name) ...".

[27] In a short essay that summarizes some crucial points of his own poetics, Bàino calls "formichizzazione della persona", that is an "ant-ification of the person," the same attitude toward the lyrical I advocated by Gruppo 63, which Giuliani, in the famous "Introduction" to the *Novissimi* anthology, calls "riduzione dell'io." See D'Oria, 1993: 41. "I coined, in the little poem 'Quatre-vingt-treize,' an ugly neologism that rivals the ugliness of another monstrous dialectal creature of mine (*the ant-ificantion of the person*)."

[28] Francesco Muzzioli, "Mariano Bàino," from a pamphlet distributed during the award ceremony of the Premio Feronia 2002, under the heading "I vincitori della passata edizione," that is "Last year's winners," sent to me by Bàino; here is the Italian: "È un Pinocchio plurilinguista, questo di Bàino, non solo perché è riletto 'da parte partenopea' (l'autore lo conosciamo come uno dei rappresentanti più interessanti e vivaci della poesia di ricerca a Napoli), ma anche perché viene accostato attraverso un impasto linguistico che va dalla parlata dialettale al recupero colto, passando per

l'invenzione verbale, il gioco di parole (da cocomero, ad esempio, deriva 'cocco omerico') e – cara all'autore sopra ogni altra – la manipolazione maccheronica improntata allo spagnolo, da hidalgo decaduto e da cerimonia 'bassa', come si addice a una riscrittura parodistica. Fino alla teatralità vera e propria: non per nulla l'episodio che resta più vicino al testo d'origine è quello di Mangiafuoco, dove tutti i personaggi prendono per sé la battuta, il 'ruolo principale' e la posa più 'plateale'."

[29] Ibidem, here is the original: "La stessa estensione instabile che, nell'originale, aveva il naso del protagonista, qui si attaglia al verso che oscilla quanto alla lunghezza del suo passo. Alternandosi almeno tre tipologie: la scrittura di strofe brevi, orizzontale nella pagina; la scrittura a verso lungo con pause (segnate da curiose parentesi vuote, corrispondenti quindi a silenzi) disposta verticalmente nella pagina, che ospita di preferenza il controcanto; la prosa in carattere più piccolo che contiene la parte di commento – il meta-racconto – in cui l'autore fa il verso a se stesso, 'neocollodi di turno', ridotto a lasciare pezzi incompiuti e appunti 'allo sbaraglio', e che infine si 'dimette' con una ironica presa di distanza, abbandonando il narratore nel mentre lo oggettiva in una terza persona (ma chi scrive qui allora? Paradossi della scrittura…)."

[30] Ibidem, "Le 'moviole', che Bàino ha inserito in parentesi accanto al nome del suo archetipo riscritto, vogliono ricordare che il principio sovrano resta quello del montaggio. Il montaggio, eredità 'forte' del modernismo novecentesco, è qui a presiedere il gioco di scarti, sovrimpressioni, slittamenti e incroci di questa iperletteratura impazzita. Attraverso il gioco dei passaggi da un pezzo all'altro, intravediamo qualcosa che ci riguarda da vicino: ciò che il testo indica allegoricamente nello 'storto legno che siamo'.

Works Cited

Alfano G., Pinocchio di Baino: il burattino diventa adulto. *Il Mattino*, 24 dicembre 2000, 26.
Bàino M. (1993a), *Fax giallo*. Nola: Il laboratorio.
Bàino, M. (1993b), Quatre-vingt-treize. In: D'Oria MG (ed) *Gruppo 93: Le tendenze attuali della poesia e della narrativa: Antologia di testi teorici e letterari*. Lecce: Manni, pp. 93-94.
Bàino, M. (1994), *Ônne 'e terra*. Napoli: Pironti; then republished as Bàino, M. (2003), *Ônne 'e terra*. Civitella in val di Chiana: Zona.
Bàino, M. (2000), *Pinocchio (moviole)*. Lecce: Manni.
Bàino, M. (2001) *Fax giallo*. Arezzo: Zona.
Berisso M., Cademartori P., Casersa G. *et al.* (1993), Un autoritratto (e alcune parole notevoli). In: D'Oria M.G. (ed), *Gruppo 93. Gruppo 93: Le tendenze attuali della poesia e della narrativa. Antologia di testi teorici e letterari*. Lecce: Manni, pp. 29-38.
Bettini F. and Sanguineti E. (1983), Il piccolo fatto vero. In: *Rinascita*, 16 settembre 1983; then republished in: *Terza Ondata: Il Nuovo Movimento della Scrittura in Italia*. Bologna: Synergon, pp. 266-271.
Bettini F. and Muzzioli F. (ed.) (1990), *Gruppo '93: La recente avventura del dibattito letterario in Italia*. Lecce: Manni.
Bettini F. and Di Marco R. (ed.) (1993), *Terza Ondata: Il Nuovo Movimento della Scrittura in Italia*. Bologna: Synergon.
Carlino M. and Mastropasqua A. (1993), Notes to Mariano Baino. In: Bettini F. and Muzzioli F. (eds), *Terza Ondata. Il Nuovo Movimento della Scrittura in Italia*. Bologna: Synergon, pp. 105-106.
Cataldi P. (1994), Il conflitto delle poetiche: postmoderno *versus* allegorismo. In: *Le idee della Letteratura: Storia delle poetiche italiane del Novecento*, Roma: La Nuova Italiana Scientifica, pp. 174-192.
D'Oria A.G. (ed.) (1993), *Gruppo 93: Le tendenze attuali della poesia e della narrativa. Antologia di testi teorici e letterari*. Lecce: Manni.
Luperini R. (1994), Postmoderno critico? Discutiamone. *Baldus* 1: 29-31.
Mastropasqua A. (1993), Il "Gruppo '93": un passaggio obbligato. Dal dibattito al movimento letterario. In: Bettini F. and Muzzioli F. (eds.), *Terza Ondata: Il Nuovo Movimento della Scrittura in Italia*. Bologna: Synergon, pp. 74-77.

Ottonieri T. (ed.) (1992), *L'anello che non tiene: Poesia, Oltre-modernità, Antagonismo*. Reggio Emilia: Edizioni Elytra.

Paghi A. (1994), Il disagio del testo: Quattro letture di poesia di ricerca. *Baldus* 3-4: 66-68.

Petrella A. (ed.) (2010), *Gruppo 93: L'antologia poetica*. Arezzo: Zona.

Pontiggia G. and Di Mauro E. (1978), *La parola innamorata: I poeti nuovi: 1976-1978*. Milano: Feltrinelli.

Renello G.P. (1993), Note in margine al convegno di Reggio Emilia. *Baldus* 3-4: 24-34.

Santini F. (2013), *Io era una bella figura una volta: Viaggio nella poesia di ricerca del secondo Novecento*. Piacenza: Scritture.

Sarzana P. (1995), Napoli e le città del mondo nella poesia di Mariano Bàino, *Studi Novecenteschi* 22 (49): 247-254.

Schiffrin A. (2000), *The Business of Books: How International Conglomerates Took Over Publishing and Changed the Way We Read*. London and New York: Verso.

FAX GIALLO

YELLOW FAX

Pe una meluccia, c'averà ccostato
Mezzobbaiocco, stamo tutti a ffonno!

Giuseppe Gioachino Belli, da *Er primo bboccone* (*Sonetti*)

For a tiny apple, not worth
A buck, we've all gone belly up

Giuseppe Gioacchino Belli, from *The First Bite (Sonnets)*

va senza dirlo che si sta in deserti: vista di tartari, possibili
diversi, fumi veri non ciuffi erborei dentro
il vento e segni cose d'altri altre fatture sarebbero
degli occhi grande festa... ma non fochi non fiati
in irreale inerzia, né grido netto, né un sòn
solitario nel desierto grasso: giunglatundra intorno,
pack polare pieno d'effetti: ovunque motabronx
e paltamelma di vita in sintesi, in perdita sensoria: spappolato
spazio di silicio microchip dune d'umida
cenere e ciberpiastre cupole: nulla discorda né
scarta mai da sé, nemmeno a notte in sogno: indistanziate rive
i fiumifinti: il fax fabula il fatto che pistola xeno
in una mano e dentro le mascelle un kinomodulo,
in un imbroi di reti g, trovato morto un Gothick, trovato morto
un Kasual, tra loro in guerragiusta? e in che diversi?

it goes without saying we live in deserts: a view for tartars, possible
different, real fumes not tufts of weed inside
the wind and signs things of others other spells would bring
great pleasure to the eyes… but neither breath nor fires
in an unreal inertia, nor a sharp cry, nor a solitary
sound in the fat desert: jungletundra all around,
polar pack filled with consequences: everywhere mudbronx
and scumfilth of life in summary, sensory deprived: smashed
space of silicon microchip dunes of humid
ashes and cyber-sheet domes: nothing disagrees nor
swerves of its own accord, not even at night in dream: undistanced shores,
the fakerivers: the fax fabula the fact that guns xeno
in one hand and inside the jaws of a kinomodule,
in a tangle of g nets, a Gothik found dead,
a Kasual found dead, a justwar between them? and different how?

sotto il cielo truvuliato in nerofumo, in nembi di tempesta
   o come pinto di cilestro lindo... si guata l'horizon
da gufidiurni nottole falchilinci: d'imbianco, in un momento
   e mezzo il sole vivacalce zenita, ruzzola l'orecchie
d'acufeni (esaminar di fino anche la vampa delle vene proprie,
la pampa fondocupa dell'udito): c'è chi s'allamana d'ammansa
s'ellemene d'emmense d'imminsi s'illimini s'ollomono
d'ommonso d'ummunsu s'ullumunu col core in rogo di chi crede
:il fax favella di Baubas Baubis Bebon Belili Belfegor Babbar
   Bagoe Barin Barbatus Baste Bendis Baal Baal-Gad Baal-Hammon
      ed altri Baal: l'indugio lungo, l'aspettar lo strànio
l'alieno foresto... già sai: ciascogni attesa ha un salutifero
tot (se ti sospendi?), e un tot malato (del laborinto istesso
   che ti profila il tempo?): cecaggine è più spesso,
non vedere fronda, se i cerchiosi (gli anelli, in lingua

under a turmoiled sky filled with soot, stormy billows
      or as painted with pristine azure... gazing at the orizzonte
    like dayowls noctules lynxhawks: 'ofasudden, in a second
      and a half the stonelime sun zeniths, tumbles the ears
from tinnitus (also closely examine your vein's flame,
the bottomdark pampas of the hearing): ammansata anlaghtans some
  emmensete enleghtens inlightins immimsiti ommonsoto
onloghtons ummunsutu unlughtuns* with the heart on the stake of those who believe
:the fax tells of Baubas Baubis Bebon Belili Belfegor Babbar
    Bagoe Barin Barbatus Baste Bendis Baal Baal-Gad Baal-Hammon
      and other Baals: the long hesitation, the wait for the strainger
the foreign alien... you know: eachevery delay has a salvific
modicum (if you're suspended?), and a sickly modicum (for the very labyrinth
    time itself lays out for you?): blindity is more often than not,
being incapable of seeing foliage, if the circlous (the rings, the zargon

---

* The Italian plays with the famous poem by Ungaretti "M'illumino d'immenso," which could be translated as "Immensity enlightens me." The vowels are all progressively substituted with "a," "e," "i," "o," and "u." (translator's note)

zerga) del tener pazienza l'uno appresso all'altro
si spupillano... già sai la croce di un séipse in usanza
di bislunga, d'incocciosa attesa (farsi l'arnesi per fare
di séipse e d'altri sé la prova e l'esperienza, o farsi
tibie coccia femori ed altr'ossi): e supponiamo la volta
del chiattendetrova, pure in poco scorcio, in 7 stente
sillabe parodiche: m'imbuio di limitato... delle cose che per
senso nostro luce non prendono (diciamo un cielo nero, un nero
specchio, una nessuna luce) e in tali cose un dislegarsi pieno
dei colori: un non-acume del bianco, non votato
ai nientamenti torbidi di oscure trasparenze, né ingolfato
nel senzacolore... farfalloso fax, di che farfugli? di
Cleopatra? Cleopatra non sarebbe stata bianca? una Cleopatra
neeeeeeeeeeeeeeeeeeeeeeeeeeeeeeeeeeeeeeeeeeeeeeeegra?
ne ra?

language) of staying patient one after the next
they depupil themselves... you know the crux of seipse in the stead
of twicelong, insharded delay (to build the tools to test
seipse and other selves and try them, or build
tibias coccyges femurs and other bones): and let's pretend for the sake
of thosewhowaitfind, and yet in a small span, in 7 shriveled
parodic syllables: limitation darkens me... about those things that through our
senses don't come to light (let's say a black sky, a black
mirror, a non-light) and in these things a complete undoing
of colors: a non-acumen in the white, not inclined to
the torbid nullments of dark transparencies, nor stuck
in the colorless... butterflyish fax, what are you mumbling about?
Cleopatra? What do you mean Cleopatra wasn't white? A Cleopatra who's
neeeeeeeeeeeeeeeeeeeeeeeeeeeeeeeeeeeeeeeeeeeeeeeeeeeegro?
    bla   ck?

come l'adesso di questa luce: luminello novo o suo no
suo inverso e cuntré, contraddanza in dirupati
spazi, in supraffigi ov'è sinistro di vetriera,
scena di archi infinitivi, orrido a noi dimora in qualche
chiocciola di tempo (dove il cappero imparò l'aroma
e buscò il tono suo verdeveleno, dove il tordo navigò
esordiente, un'ala alida infra l'onda, l'altra al vento,
come vela, nocchiero perché stracco (e in Partenope ebbe nome
di marvizzo, quasi al mare avvezzo)): il fax fila, fa bianche
bave, baffi di nullaggine nel testo, stento
leggere di pelle crasticata morduta fatta pel(l)e d'altra (p)elle
um(a)na... (u)mano... (s)acr(ifi)cio (qui una gran pillacchera
bianchiccia vuota non leggibile) ( ) in cima alle pi(ram)idi (a)
zteche (qui viene una riga molto mozza) cro(cef)isse
( ) v(it)time... scoi(a)te anc(or)a (v)ive... sace(rdo)ti le (in)dos

like the now of this light: new lightwhirl or its no
    its opposite and contraire, quadrille in impervious
        spaces, in overfigures where there's a glass factory accident,
    scene of infinitive arches, horror to us an abode in some
        snail of time (where the caper learned the aroma
        and got its greenpoison tone, where the thrush crossed
    the first time, an arid wing through the wave, the other in the wind,
like a sail, a pilot from fatigue (and in Partenope was called
    redwing, as in used to the sea)): the fax runs, foams
        white, whiskers of nothingness in the text, weak
reading of chewed up skin bitten made into s(k)in of other hum(a)n
    (s)kin... (h)uman... (s)acr(ifi)ce (here a whole lot of whitish
empty illegible splatter) ( ) on top of the py(ram)ids (a)
    ztec (here comes a stump of a line) cru(cif)ied
    ( ) v(ic)tims... fl(a)yed sti(l)l (a)live... the pri(es)ts (wo)re

(s)avano (   ) gran macula s'ingolla il resto, salvo
    (   ) giag(ua)ro rosso... pi(u)mato serpe... glifi del calen(d)ario
    (   ) fibrilla il fax: l'umanità l'umane genti ttinsieme sui 5
virgola 5 miliardi di caccoli ghigni pupi cazzimatti avanti
    in regress alla ritmica dell'un virgola 7 per cento ognanno
        ttinsieme a capofitto incontro alle schififiche
            sorti e regressive con arrivo ai sogli del 2000 in 6 virgola
2   miliardi di zomàrizombie in un ronzare oblioso
del perché l'asciuttamento d'occhi, del percome gli occhi
sono sciutti quali anfore mùmmare langelle senza un flusciu d'acqua
    :ttinsieme essendo o essendo stati un altro paio di maniche
        essendo come la moglie di cesare la gatta nel sacco
    in una torre d'avorio essendoci rivisti a filippi cavoli salvando
    e capra insalutati ospiti essendo al cielo 7° in una ferrea
    botte essendo stati sulle spine prendendo papere cantonate a

them (   ) great macula swallows the rest, except
   (   ) red jag(ua)r... f(ea)thered serpent... calen(d)ar glyphs
   (   ) the fax fibrillates: the humanity the human peoples altoggether around 5 point 5 billion boogers grins babies crazydicks forward
      in regress to the rhythm of the one point 7 percent every year
         altoggether headfirst toward the grossific
         and regressive destiny projected for the dawn of 2000 at 6 point
2   billion zonkeyzombies in a forgetful buzz
 of why the drying of eyes, how the eyes
    are dry like amphorae wineskins pitchers without a drop of water
         :altoggether being or having been a horse of a different color
            being like caesar's wife cat in the bag
      in an ivory tower meeting at high noon having your cake
   and eating it too being ungreeted guests on cloud 9 on solid
   ground having been on pins and needles causing blunders duped into

regger moccoli essendo stati piantati in asso avendo preso
granchi menando il can per l'aia l'orso a modena potendo
mangiare a ufo nascere in camiciola legandosela al dito levando
dal foco castagne pillole dorando subendo o avendo
subìto di tantalo il supplizio facendo fatiche d'ercole
facendo come l'asino di buridano cavalli essendo di battaglia
sul libro nero essendo sotto l'egida entrandoci come culo con
le quarantore come pomo della discordia come gioco che non
vale la candela pagando ché pantalone paga paganini
non ripete parlando di corda in casa d'impiccato perdendo
tramontane piangendo lacrime di lacoste perdendo alla
martin la cappa per un punto essendo o essendo stati presi in
contropiede rimandando adcalendasgraecas sciogliendo nodi
gordiani facendo autodafé una fatica di sisifo: il fax
ci s'inframmischia, frascheggia di un passare il quarto d'ora

being the third wheel having been stood up having barked up
    the wrong tree beating around the bush leading a horse to water
eating on someone else's dime born with a silver spoon bearing a grudge pulling
      chestnuts out of the fire sugarcoating it enduring or having
endured tantalus' punishment the labors of hercules
acting like buridan's ass being pieces de resistance
on the black list being under the aegis fish out
    of water like the apple of discord not worth the paper
        it's written on footing the bill paganini
    doesn't repeat speaking of rope in the house of the hanged losing
the bearings crying lacoste tears close
  but no cigar being or having been caught
      off guard waiting till kingdom come undoing Gordian
knots burning at stake enduring sisyphus punishment: the fax
gets tangled up in it, rustles for a whole fifteen minutes

di Rabelais e e sao ke in keste terre in kesta skakkierata terra
ninfe non sono tornate, le ninnélle nigne ninfepupille ite
partite fuìte fuggite fugate siderate per sempre
sideree in vasti gurgiti di blu: nella scafarda
che diresti il mondo restano poppoli ruzzano prosappie
schiattano schiatte si scamazzano alla guisa degli arcaici
archiparenti, fallocefali col dubbio se è l'amore
che va odiato o se è l'odio che va amato (come scimie
grattarole in testa, come cherubbinieri in barzellette): hiù
i poppoli dell'ovest, i westpoppoli del tedio,
i malinconici spleenici d'historia artefici (fisima
il fax, flussiona di naziskin australiani: ispirati un poco agli
hooligans inglesi, teen-ager è il ritratto base, vario background
dietro le spalle: odiato molto l'immigrato vietnamita e poco
l'aborigeno (non degno d'odio nazi)): e poppoli con cervella

of Rabelais and Ich wit that in these landes in this checker'd lande
nymphs haven't returned, the itseebitsee tiney nymphpupils gone
left fled escaped snatched frozen forever
sidereal in vast gurgitations of blue: in the saddle
you'd call the world peopples remain kinnfolk romp
lineages kick the bucket get trampled like the archaic
archrelatives, phallocephalous unsure whether it's love
that should be hated or it's hate that should be loved (like monkeys
with pruriginous heads, like cherubaneers in a joke): 'nough
the peopples of the west, the westernpeopples of boredom,
the splenic melancholics makers of history (a fixation
the fax, flushes from Australian naziskin: slightly inspired by
English hooligans, teen-ager being the basic idea, various backgrounds
behind them: having hated the Vietnamese immigrant a lot and the
aboriginal a little (unworthy of nazi hate)): and peopples with brains

abarbagliate e grosse, i tribaloidi poppoli, i natura, i senza
historia, gliumanisoloallazoologica, quelli
che a ragione ci eserciti dominio, come su animali (benedetto Hegel...
benedetto Croce): eunsangiorgio nella testa, co' la testa
sangiorgiuta contro i mostri, lancia avversa al pappagnacco
drago che fa con monnavergine il milordo il farinello il male
in figura d'un orribil moro o sotto quella d'un orribil
moro (fare il conto de li cunti dei dimònii apparsi, diaboli,
farfarelli): fumiga il fax di scimmiamadre moresolito portante
in giro sua creatura morta fino a che non c'è il disgrego
e lo sminuzzo: ed è perché le bestie non se l'affigurano
la morte (e nell'umano svolgersi è figura fresca, quasi fresca,
quasi recente)... sorride agresto in afropop tarocco mister
Venerdì: nous autres civilisations, nous savons maintenant
que nous sommes mortelles: sorride mesto mister Robinson

bewildered and big, the tribaloid peopples, the nature ones, the ones without
    historia, humansasseenbyzoology, those
whom you're right to treat as subjects, like animals (blessed Hegel...
    blessed benedetto Croce): andasaintgeorge in the head, with a saint georged
    head against the monsters, spear pointed at the whole dragon
        thing that acts like a milord a rascal with the youngmaiden, the picture
        of evil of a horrible moor or under that of a horrible
    moor (the tally of tales of demons appeared, devils,
farfarelli): the fax fumigates with monkeymother asperusual parading
        about its dead offspring until there's the unraveling
            and the mincing: and it's because the beasts don't visualize
death (and in the human unfolding is fresh image, somewhat fresh,
        somewhat recent)... mister Friday smiles rustically in an afropop
    tarot: nous autres civilisations, nous savons maintenant
            que nous sommes mortelles: mister Robinson smiles sadly

nel suo tarocco un po' nebbiato pampaniato po' polvere
eombrasiamo po' timeodanaos et donaferentes: ride agresto
Sancho Panza in taroccuccio suo: dos linajes solos due sole
razze hay en el mundo, decìa mi' nonna, que son
el tener y el no tener... poi come da scissura non vedi vedi
un arruffato trasmodar di nuvole: il tarocco dove Dino
Campana poetò la pampa da infrenabile treno nella notte,
a cielo pieno di cavalli sorti dal livido teschione della luna,
corsieri aizzati da fulminei cavalieri indiani, fulminei vivi
e morti (le code di lucertole dei muri...) a dire, acuti,
in lance, che non v'è poppolo pargolo e si cresce anche senza
diario... (figlia il fax un fogliolino; a Osaka specchi e raggi
laser deviano in traiettorie a zeta tuoni e fulmini (un'eterna
estate?)) in corsa urlando fra nitriti a un'illusione
d'universo che dicembre december è per loro la luna

in his tarot, a bit foggy, thick with dust
andshadowsweare a bit timeodanaos et donaferentes: Sancho Panza
smiles rustically in his little tarot: dos linajes solos only two
races hay en el mundo, decìa my nana, que son
el tener y el no tener... then as if through a fissure you don't see see
a disheveled transmodification of clouds: the tarot where Dino
Campana sang the pampas from an unstoppable train at night,
under a sky filled with horses born of the moon's livid skull,
steed spurred by lightning fast Indian horsemen, lightning fast dead
and alive (the lizard tails of the walls...) that's to say, acute,
with spears, since there are no childish peopples and one can even grow up
without a diary... (the fax births a little sheet: in Osaka laser beam and
mirrors redirect thunder and lightning in z trajectories (an endless
summer?)) running screaming over the neighs at an illusion
of universe that dicembre December to them is the moon

degli alberi scoppiettanti e june giugno si chiama nellaluna cheingrassa... riversati dalla coppa dei massacri in una grandine obliqua di galoppi... a ripercorrere su neri bianchi sauri roani bai la buona terra, a dire il dire della freccia zigzaghella libera fra l'arte di spostarsi e di restare... ra ffica il fax di un fax partito da Bolzanobaridabologna: al Melkwelgcoffee al chiostro di Rockzilla in sede Wakantanka (pre sso campo schettinaggio) ragamuffin reggae hip hop rap sound system in un vento a sud di marx a est di hitler a nord di blade runner a ovest del kitsch... cinzanino e sangue e se arride del concorso il bollino sotto il tappo via da cagnabaldi via da accattosi ed affarfanti via da affarinati via d'attremanti su su con nuova mente nuovo deck e nuovo vuoto nuovo microsoft dietro l'orecchio dentro il rumor bianco in pozzi gravitanti diddiolavoce... più del bacio di Moll, la laida Moll, Moll

of the crackling trees and June giugno is called inthemoon
thatfattens... poured from the cup of massacres in the oblique
    hail of cavalcades... re-traversing the good earth on white
      sorrel roan bay horses, to talk the talk of the zigzagey
    arrow free to choose between the art of moving and staying put... bur
sting the fax of a fax sent from Bolzanobarifrombologna: to
Melkwelgcoffee to the Rockzilla cloister to the seat of Wakantanka (by
  the skate park) ragamuffin reggae hip hop rap
sound system in a wind south of marx east of hitler north of
  blade runner west of kitsch... a shot of cinzano and blood and if
the contest under the bottle cap is favorable no more bushpigs
  no more rubes no more cooters no more gritters no more scoffers
    up up with a new mind a new deck a new emptiness a new microsoft
      behind the ear inside the white noise inside gravitational wells
    thevoiceofgod... even more than Moll's kiss, lurid Moll, Moll

dai due orecchini a forma di gesù macheperleisonoiladroni: "Gesù
lo porto in bocca", e porta in su, polliceindice, il labbrone sco
perchiando l'unica infrazione alle gengive: ildenterottoegiallo
ilcaninotrapanato a mo' di crocefisso... un quissimile dei cristi
di Unamuno, pazzissimi di croce per sperare pasque per
fiatare agonie nelle zampogne, per dire in canto, insanguinati
esangui la nascita africana, a Tangeri... e come smorfiarono
paonazzi lividi in rètine di tori, nei quadrupedi
altricristi in Spagna, non glauchi di rinascita sui carri
di trionfo altrui, stecchita grafica stagliata sulla rossa
sera sotto ilmortomotorenonmosso... soffia il fax: il racket
del pomodoro oro rosso: liremille a quintale e terra
di Capitanata fa una resa annua di 16.000.000 di quintali... poi
risoffia di giumente andate a sbattere insuicidinmassa... malate
strane di tossine nel cervello o d'abuso di trifoglio: testabassa

with the two earrings shaped like jesus butthatforherarethethieves: "I keep
 Jesus in my mouth," and purses, thumbindex, the big lip un
  covering the only infraction to her gums: thebrokenyellowtooth
 thedrilledcanine in the form of a cross... sumptin' like the christs
   of Unamuno, crazy about the cross hoping for easters
   breathing the bagpipes' agonies, to say in song, bloodstained
    bloodless the African birth, in Tangiers... and how they grimaced
     flushed livid in bulls' retinas, in the otherchrist
   quadrupeds in Spain, not glaucous from rebirth on the chariots
    of another's triumph, dead as a graphic doornail set against the red
 evening under thedeadunmovedmotor... rustles the fax: the red gold
      tomato racket: lirasathousand per quintal and the land
   of Capitanata yields 16,000,000 quintals per year... and then rustles
   again with mares gone to crash inmasssuicide... strangely
  sick with toxins in their brain or for abusing the clover: headdown

e schianto in faccia all'albero alla roccia, lo zoccolo raspando calmo in finitura, dolcemente... fu per sogno di zucche rotolanti dal pendio senza spaccarsi senza dar pastocchi all'erba peperella e irrequiete verdiacrobate nel salto del vallone a ciàffete nel mare schizzichiando, riemergendo albatre bianche uccelle erratiche per sempre... eh, la stagnola del mare, l'antica pena corale delle onde, vastità non più coperchio a nulla, memoria azzurra d'elefante che rivanga senza posa i franamenti dell'ossosa terra... broncio immane, immane distensione ravvivante i gocciolanti umani che ne emergono, vispi mentre inspirano la brezza che saranno, il loro fumo futuro... il fax fuffigna di un folle detenuto a Waupun, nel Wisconsin, dai 20 personaggi 20in giostra fra le tempie, senza che un pizzardone un flik dell'intracranico faccia da capataz caudillotrainer faccia da

....

and slam in the face of the tree of the rock, filing the hoof
calm in a finishing touch, tenderly... it was for a dream of pumpkins rolling
    down hill without breaking without messing up the pepper
    grass and restless greenacrobate in the leap across the ditch and
    plopping in the splashing sea, re-emerging white albatrosses
forever wandering birds... eh, the sea's aluminum foil, the ancient
    choral pain of the waves, expanse no longer lid to anything,
    blue elephant memory that endlessly rehashes the crumblings
of the boney earth... immense frown, immense distension reviving
    the dripping humans emerging from it, sprightly as they inhale
    the breeze they'll become, their future smoke ... the fax fumbles something
    about a madman convicted in Waupan, in Wisconsin, with 20 personalities
20 circling between his temples, without a traffic cop a billy club
    of the interskull acting as chieftain caudillotrainer acting as
    ....

leaderguru duxcondùcator che scotenni e manduchi ur-cannibale gl'altr'ji sull' orlo della disputa, au fond des solitudes, fora de limini de tempospazio, in fonico tessuto di canee : un vocetruce a dare panalpane e vinavil nastradesivi al cosmococcico d'oggetti che si sfanno in un raggriccio iccio che non preservano le ruggini uggini d'un ideuzza loro di du rata ata... un dio dei nodi ch'iteri il richiamo, un azionista di riferimento per la mente d'1 niuno e una ventina... informa il fax d'un bel balfino nato in vascacquatile di Kioto o Tokio: avrà più dei 2 metri e 9 di papà delfino, ché maman balena è lunga cinque (e scorcia pinne e zinne ad usum, come dir?, Balphini): e che tu vada a spigole, se vuoi, in tirrene mucillagini: la balfigola prole in lunghi corridoi di sottomare si districhi e diporti, illesa fra i silenti monnezzai profondi, il cellulòideo occhio ponderante quanto scherma la medusa

leaderguru duxcondùcator to skin and manducate ur-cannibal
the others on the brink of dispute, au fond des solitudes,
outside the boundaries of timespace, in a phonic texture of ruckus
: a cruelvoice spicandspanning and magic glue and tape
for the cosmospieces of objects that come apart in a shrinking inking
that don't save the rusts hust of a tiny idea of theirs in two
installments almonds... a god of knots who repeats the calling, a key
stockholder in the mind of 1 no one and twenty people... the fax
informs about a nice wholphin born in a waterytank in Kyoto or To
kyo: will be longer than his father dolphin's 2 point 9 meters, for maman
whale is five meters long (and cut fins and tits ad usum, shall we say?
Wholphini): and may you fish for seabass, if you want, amid Tyrrhenian
mucilage: may the wholphigolous offspring disentangle and sail through long
underwater corridors, unscathed through silent deep dumpsters,
the celluloid-like eye pondering what the jellyfish hides

(umbrella di mendicante, giostra fosforescente di cavalluzzi
marini), come t'intana la primavera metallizzata dei coralli,
il mucchio d'ostriche (cofano di sputi e perle), quanto si
latita tra l'oloturie (di cenciaiuolo verminosi sacchi),
dietro l'attinia (insanguinato ceppo ove lasciarono capelli
serpini sirene decapitate), in mezzo ai verdi vermi
delle alghe, dietro quel cassettone o nella stanza di là,
sotto il letto dichiscrissedimare... la balfigola diosalvi
dalpalombaroboiasottomarinoacrobataprofondoburattino
nelteatromutodeipescispauracchiobecchinomascheratuomopneumatico
che aiuta con l'arpione l'infinito ad essere... il cruento
cugino mare... dal fax affiora fievole la nota di una diaspora
: via tutti dalla Twentieth... Century Fox... il ritmo vasto
dell'esistere, in onde contrarie che si scontrano, in ublique
dinastie d'onde trasverse... nu poco 'e bbene e nu poco e male

(beggar's ombrella, phosphorescent merry-go-round of sea
    horsies), how it dens you the metallic spring of corals,
the pile of oysters (trunk of spit and pearls), when someone's
      wanted among sea cucumbers (worm-ridden sacks of rag-and-bone man),
  behind sea anemones (bloody trunk where decapitated sirens
        left their serpent hair), amid the green worms
of seaweed, behind that chest or in that room over there,
    under the bed ofthosewhowroteofthesea... the wholphigolous godsaveus
    fromthedeepdiverunderwaterexecutionerdeepacrobatemarionette
inthesilenttheateroffishboogiemanundertakermaskedpneumaticman
      who helps the infinite harpoon to be... the gory
sea cousin... from the fax dimly surfaces the note of a diaspora
  : everyone out of the Twentieth... Century Fox... the vast rhythm
      of existing, in opposite waves that clash, in oblique
    dynasties of traverse waves... a bit of good and a bit of bad

fanno 'a varca navecare... luna rossa viento gruosso luna chiara bontiempo 'e mare luna avvelata acqua appreparata : a Capu Horn si gire gira ma si nu' gire torna a jì contra currente nunn'è fatica 'e niente nun truove pe' mmare taverne è traretòra l'acqua manza e fauza nei letti dei venti a bordeggià... un cielo e un mare belli, belli tanto che avresti detto che non c'erano: d'imbianco il viso ai pesci, giù coi padri profondi di maree (filosofanti al sole, sapida di sale greco la lingua)... naviganti... tolti via dall'onda, sparafondati da un fistivuli vento fatto scattacori, nei denti un 'affanculo prima del primo sorso e a taglio le pupille, non camposàntea carne per topi tra patate... ciao grande i delfaroversocasa... il fax filologa che "jean" deforma Genova e che a Genova la stoffa mitica dei jeans fu ordita e fu tramata... Jeangenova destinata di avere agli occhi l'ago che declina dalla stella per non poco

make the ship sail ahead... red moon strong wind pale
moon goodweather at sea veiled moon prepped water
: if going to Cape Horn turn but if not go back going against
the current it's not quick work at sea you're on
your own it's treacherous that false bovine water in the winds' beds
when tacking... beautiful sky and sea, so beautiful you would have said
they weren't there: 'ofasudden white the face of the fish, down with the deep
fathers of tides (philosophizing in the sun, tongue sapid with
Greek salt)... sailors... taking away from the wave, downcast
by a festive wind turned heartthrob, a fuckoff through the teeth
before the first sip and slit pupils, non cemeterial flesh
formiceamidpotatoes...greatciaotheofthehomewardlighthouse...thefax
philologizes that "jean" corrupts Genoa and that in Genoa the mythical
fabric of jeans was wefted and warped... Jeangenoa destined
to have in its eyes the needle descending from the star for not much

spazio verso ponente... terra... terra... paese oltre l'Oceano salutato in un zoffio una favilla un fiàt: subito sera, anche sera del testo anche sera d'oceani cartacei anche sera Johannes Gensfleisch detto Gutenberg... saluti vecchio 'ceano loquace e messo muto a derivare ambasciateambasce tra le carte di chi viene verga va... fogli sui fogli... di padrinfiglio... sfoglia pure ad occhi chiusi... chimere ruminando... sfoglia... annota a margine col dito scorri con l'occhio pagine righe capriolando capitoli indici d'argomenti... el siglo siécolo che schiuppa millenario (millénaire qui meurt...) scaca suoi semi sue sfa ccimme da fior festaiolo: patullano parole papareggiano (da pa perepapesse): in broda universale agguazzano aggallan musiche mappe immagini dati&archivi virtualmente e senza fine l'i pertesto... (dal fax tafàni diafani scribillano scrivòlano: alla Volvo di Uddevalla lo vogliono devoto dell'azienda l'operaio)...

space toward the west... land ho... land ho... country beyond the Ocean
greeted with a breath a spark a fiat: night suddenly, even night
    in the text even night in the paper oceans even night Johannes
Gensfleisch a.k.a. Gutenberg... greetings y'old loquacious ocean
        and mute messenger deducting embassiesanxieties amid the papers
of those who come sign go... leaf after leaf... from fathertoson... leaf
    even with eyes shut... chimeras ruminating... leaf... note
in the margins with finger scan with eyes pages lines somersaulting
    chapters tables of contents... el siglo siécolo that kicks the bucket
        millenary (millénaire qui meurt) dumps his seeds his
cum of festive flower: they ridicule words wallowing (like po
    pishducks) : in a universal broth splash float music
        maps images data&archives virtually and without end the hy
    pertext... (from the fax scribrilliant diaphanous gnats slide: at
        Volvo in Uddevalla the worker they want him devoted to the company)...

...e fra procelle di linee fra crespe di pelle in calzante
gommaresina di mondi combinabili si evolve si adatta nel mix
in calzanti procelle di mondi di clics il ditocchio ha inter
facce di organo nuovo del dopo le schede ed i mouse i computer
del dopo il videare di Silicon Valley in gommaresina di linee
combinabili in crespe di mondi si evolve di pelle in calzanti
facce di organo mix in procelle di mondi il ditocchio di clics
ha interfacce del dopo del dopo Silicon Valley in gommaresina
di facce ha interfacce di organo nuovo del dopo le schede
ed i mouse videare calzante si adatta in procelle di pelle
ti chiede son'io l'unnomongolo atroce contrario alla vita
così nuovo e clonale? iperlibroreo che abbrustola abbrucia
da attila la vecchia tecnica dotta?... outputta il fax, gra
ffia prefetti offrendo i fatti di una nera pantera d'una jatta
c"o pilo annegrecato che gattigna scappa scapola per boschi

... and amid tempests of lines amid pleats of skin in tight
gum resin of combinable worlds evolves adapts in the mix
of tight tempests of worlds of clicks the eyefinger has inter
faces of a new organ of the after the discs and the mice the computers
of the after the videoing of Silicon Valley in gum resin of combinable
lines in pleats of worlds evolves from skin into tight
faces of organ mix of tempests of worlds the eyefinger of clicks
has interfaces of the after of the after Silicon Valley in gum resin
of faces has interfaces of a new organ of the after the discs
and the mice videoing tight adapts into tempests of skin
asking you am I the atrocious hunmongol opposed to life
so new and clone-like? hyperlibrorean who roasts burns
like attila the old erudite technique?... the fax outputs, scra
tches prefects offering the fax of a black panther of a kitty
with blackened fur that strolls runs flees through the tusco-emilian

tosco-emiliani sfilata fra gabbie prisòni, da gargiobbole
fuggita toma toma, quattaquatta da serragli: artiglio a sgriff
affilato dal Lazio al Triveneto... braccata e foresta dentando
luserte topini ma lungi da circhi e tendoni, finiti i bestiari
i zompari, finiti i fintari i clownari, stoppati castigari
e trombonari cupi, i peppeppèri i perepeppeppèri striduli
in trombazze: boscaglie, amori con leggiere lonze o forse lontre
lupi: scopari distesi (eronne eronne...): il fax profonde scrosci
d'acquagioni, friccica tifoni floridiani: piove, acidamente, il
pleut (parbleu!, après le déluge?) à verse, horizontalement
(le vent..): et ces nuages cabres se prennent à hennir
tout un univers de villes auriculaires... odi? la pioggia cade
su la solitaria verdura con un crepitìo che dura e varia
nell'aria secondo le fronde più rade, men rade... piove...
sul nulla che si fa in queste ore di sciopero generale... piove

woods cat-walking through cages prisons, escaped from
the slammer nice and easy, on the sly from the menagerie: claw ready to scratch
sharpened from Lazio to Triveneto... chased and marginalized toothing
lizards and small mice but far from circuses and tents, done with beastiaroos
the jumparoos, done with the fakaroos, the clownaroos, halted the punisharies
and the grim trumpetaries, the taratantaras the screeching taratararas
in bad trombones: brush, loves with light leopards or maybe otters
wolves: distended fuckeries (yowza yowza...): the fax effuses patters
of drownpours, flushes Floridian typhoons: it rains, acidly, the
pleut (parblue!, après le deluge?) à verse, horizontalmente
(le vent..): et ces nuages cabres se prennent à hennir
tout un univers de villes auriculaires... hear it? the rain falls
on the solitary produce with a crackling that lasts and varies
in the air according to the foliage, thick or thin... it rains...
on the nothing that gets done in these hours of general strike... it rains

sulla cartella esattoriale... ascolta, ascolta... l'accordo delle
aeree cicale a poco a poco più sordo si fa sotto il pianto
che cresce... piove... sulla greppia nazionale... un canto vi si
mesce più roco che di laggiù sale... ascolta... piove...
sulla Gazzetta Ufficiale, piove su via Solferino, e il pino
ha un suono, e il Parlamento altro suono: dal ciel cinerino piove
sull'assenza universale che il pianto australe rinfresca: chi
sa dove, chi sa dove! Qui piove di nuovo su Ermione, ma ora
da Erminia si bagna (col suo vero nome)... e metticela tu,
lector, la completezza, la soddisfazione: libera tu, lector
l'ansia del tutto che ci hai nell'occhio: genera tu
gli opposti alla tinta singola, al giallo suono unilaterale, lector,
che il fax fiascula come bile: giallosporco acidamaro della
terra, vecchio nulla di collere, colèri, lector, lector, le
ctor, col martelletto della pupilla pigialo il tasto

on the tax form... listen, listen... the harmony of the
ethereal cicadas little by little dampens and the mounting
    cry comes forth... it rains... on the national manger... a coarser
song mixed with it rising from the bottom... listen... it rains...
    on the Official Gazette, it rains on via Solferino, and the pine
has one sound, and the Parliament another: from the ashy sky it rains
    on the universal absence that the austral cry refreshes: who knows
    where, who knows where! Here it rains again on Ermione, but now
    at Erminia's she gets wet (under her real name)... and you do it,
    lector, fill in the blanks, give satisfaction: you free it, lector
    the angst for the whole you have in your eye: you make
the opposites of the single color, for the yellow a unilateral sound, lector,
    whom the fax flasks like bile: dirtyyellow bitteracid of the
    earth, old nothing of cholers, colèri, lector, lector, le
    ctor, with the hammer of the pupil press the vermillion

amariglio del mondo, il giallo nato per gioire e fattu minchia
agra: càvane rossi, blu, prova a provare spasmi nel suo corpo
crudo d'agrume, nel citrigno imposto al ghettoebreo al gialletto
prostituta, nella sua patina di umor statico, di zolfo nei
cieli gialli di lotte di sassi di zolle con domande e screzi di
nontiscordardimé, di gialla luce con sua ombra viola (en fransé
mozzarellà: magàr non è toute une boutanade il dir que il gran
problem è plus la relation col mond que le mystère du mond),
lector, e st'alkimia del dire è storia di una miatuasuanostra
vostraloro pazzeria (del tipo inventa il vocalico dei colori
: nero Aico, bianco Eico, rosso Iico, blu Oico, verde Uico),
di una mattezza di gavotta ripetuta, ripetuta dal vibrare
di metalliche lamelle titillate da un cilindro in rotazione,
dal coatto circuitare di damine e cavalieri nella musica pian
piano sempre uguali nella pena nel sorriso nel fedele tedio...

key of the world, the yellow born to rejoice and turned into a sour
   cock: draw reds, blues, try to experience spasms in its body
     raw as a citrus, in the citric imposed on the jewghetto on the yellowish
        prostitute, with its patina of static humor, of sulfur in the
yellow skies of struggles with stones with turfs with questions and squabbles
   of forgetmenots, of yellow light with its purple shade (on fronsay
     mozzarellà: maybè its not toot une bullshìt il dir that il grand
       problème is plus la relation with the mond than le mystère du mond),
lector, and this alkemy of speech is the history of a myyourhisherour
   yourtheir craziness (of the sort invented by the colors' vocalist
     : black Aicous, white Eicous, red Iicous, blue Oicous, green Uicous),
      of a madness of repeated gavotte, repeated by the vibration
        of metal gills titillated by a rotating cylinder,
     by the compulsory circuiting of dames and knights in the music ever so
slow always the same in the sorrow in the smile in the faithful boredom...

ÔNNE 'E TERRA

VRÉNZOLE*

---

* Brandelli; cose di poco conto

LAND WAVES

SHREDS*

* Scraps; things of little consequence

'O Ggeniuslò

È no perdere lo tiempo
scrivere poesie
per la cetà di Napole

Francesco Di Biondo

Et je déteste, moi, le bel azur!

Stephane Mallarmé, *Hérodiade*

(…) è inutile stabilire se Zenobia sia da
classificare tra le città felici o tra quelle
infelici. Non è in queste due specie che ha
senso dividere le città, ma in altre due:
quelle che continuano attraverso gli anni e
le mutazioni a dare la loro forma ai desideri
e quelle in cui i desideri o riescono a
cancellare la città o ne sono cancellati

Italo Calvino, *Le città invisibili*

'O Ggeniuslò

>And waste no time
>writing poems
>for the city of Naples
>
>Francesco Di Biondo

>Et je déteste, moi, le bel azur!
>
>Stephane Mallarmé, *Hérodiade*

>(…) it's useless to try and classify Zenobia
>as either a happy or unhappy city.
>Cities shouldn't be divided into these
>two types, but rather into two others:
>those that continue, over the years
>and across mutations, to shape desires
>and those in which desires either manage
>to erase the city or are erased by it
>
>Italo Calvino, *Invisible Cities*

A

a)

jute pe' ll'aria, sottencoppa, asciute d'asfardo c"a capa
'nvacanza e vacante a ffà' 'nu stracchimpacchio
'e carnumma ciacella accedetorio
a ffà maciéllo e chianca: 'na carnara
(e chelli ffoto cu "papà nun correre"): pà
pà: sottencoppa 'e ttrappulélle, ll'automobbile
a sanfasò, pe' ll'aria jute, ca tenevano 'a voglia
'e fa' tuffi 'int"o gliòmmero d"e vvie,
'e 'nzamà', c"o pazzuóteco cuórpo
ca manco 'e ttigre ll'hanno maje alcanzato...
o era 'n' ôgn"e bbelva 'a sguarratura
c"o vvì?, ll'età appalesa d"e rrammère...
'O juóco, fuje 'o juóco, fuje 'o sfizio
'e quann'esce 'a tennerumma, 'o juóco 'e ll'attimo, 'a troppa
fittezza...
'O ffulminarse, fuje,
dint"o scapizzo : ué: 'a caperitómmola
'ncopp"a ll'autostrada: p'accadenza,
scasualmente: ué: perduto
'o scemanfù 'e vernice: a ffa' ruvine zitte
overamente

A
a)
andate per aria, sottosopra, uscite dall'asfalto con la testa / in vacanza e vuota a fare una balordaggine / di carname carnina eccidio / a far macello e macelleria : un carnaio / (e quelle foto con "papà non correre"): pà / pà: sottosopra le trappolette, le automobili / a come viene, per aria andate, che avevano la voglia / di fare tuffi nel gomitolo delle strade, / di sciamare, con l'avventato corpo / che neanche le tigri hanno mai raggiunto... / o era un'unghia di belva lo squarcio / che, vedi?, l'età palese delle lamiere... / Il gioco, fu il gioco, fu il capriccio / di quando fuoriesce il tenerume, il gioco dell'attimo, la troppa / fittezza... / Il fulminarsi, fu, / nella caduta: ué : il capitombolo / sull'autostrada: /per accidente, / casualmente: ué: perduta / la boria di vernice: a far rovine zitte / veramente

A

a)

up in the air, upside-down, off the pavement mind
on vacation and empty up to no good
a carnery carnegie slaughter
butchering it as a butcher: carnage
(and those pictures with "daddy drive safe"): dad
dy: upside-down the little traps the cars
half-assed, up in the air, yearning to
dive in the tangle of streets,
to swarm, with body so hurried
not even tigers could match...
or was it the nail of a beast that tear
that, you see?, the obvious age of metal...
game, it was the game, it was a whim
of when tenderness comes out, the game of a moment, the excess
of thickness...
the flashing, was,
in the fall: ohi: the somersault
over the freeway: by accident,
by chance: ohi: having lost
the arrogance of paint: turning to silent rubble
really

b)

a struppiamiento a strusce-e-strisce a vvà trova a ccuntra ggenio
a tròsce-e-mósce a usanza a sustenuto a cuntrarià' a arrugnarse e a struscenarse

b)
a storpiamento a strusce-e-strisce a chi lo sa a contra / ggenio / a pronto-e-chiaro a usanza a sostenuto a contrariare a contrarsi / e a strofinarsi

b)

by botching it by fits and starts by go figure by twisted arm
by hippity hoppity by usage by sustenance by contrary by shrinking and by scratching

a)
Pitaffio degl'impiccati

se avrete per noi indurito cuore
oj frate umane,
ormaje
nun ce ne 'mporta...
si rida pure
della sventura nostra, della pioggia
che ci liscivia e lava,
su, ridete
'e ll'uócchie sbrandellati dalle orbite,
del bel lavoro fattoci dai corvi,
ca pilo pilo ciglia ciglia hanno sgrassato
'o cranio, e jà', rerìte
del ballo senza posa dint"o viénto...
ormai
nulla c'importa, né c'è
qui scherzo o scherno,
ma ditece,
diteci, sì?, fratelli umani: cosa
di più ci ha uccisi: il riso,
la pietà,
un insoffribile disgusto?

a)
Epitaffio degli impiccati
se avrete per noi indurito cuore / o fratelli umani, / ormai / non ce ne importa... / si rida pure / della sventura nostra, della pioggia / che ci liscivia e lava, / su, ridete / degli occhi sbrandellati dalle orbite, / del bel lavoro fattoci dai corvi, / che pelo a pelo ciglia a ciglia hanno sgrassato / il cranio, suvvia, ridete / del ballo senza posa nel vento.../ ormai / nulla c'importa, né c'è / qui scherzo o scherno, / ma diteci, / diteci, sì?, fratelli umani: cosa / di più ci ha uccisi: il riso, / la pietà, / un insoffribile disgusto?

a)
Hangmen's Epitaph

oh human brothers, if you've hardened
your heart on our account,
by now
we don't care...
go ahead and laugh
at our misfortune, at the rain
that licks and lyes us,
c'mon, laugh
at eyes unraveled from sockets
at the nice work the crows have done,
hair by hair lash by lash have trimmed
our skull, c'mon, laugh
at our endless dance in the wind...
by now
nothing matters, nor is there
joking nor mocking,
but tell us,
tell us, yes?, human brothers: what
killed us the most: laughter,
pity,
an unbearable disgust?

B

a)

'nu juôco a ccaselle, 'na specie
'e juôco d"a papera, 'o ssà?,
ca se chiamma *monapoli*: dadi,
dduje dadi, d"e dadi
'nduvina tu 'o scopo,
si tèneno scopo,
si arrivano 'a casa cu ll'albero
'e pino, 'nduvina
si avanza, si arrèteca 'o cielo
celeste azzurrato,
si 'o jolly
ce sta, e si 'o fa
Pulcinella
'nduvina
'nduvina pecché 'sti ccaselle
pe' smatamòrfia
'na scàtula só'
e p"o finale
ogni cosa ce zompa,
ce zompano 'e dadi, 'e dduje dadi c"o scopo,
si tèneno scopo,
e 'a casa cu ll'albero
'e pino, e 'a zeffunno
'int"a scàtula 'o cielo
azzurrato celeste
c'arrèteca o avanza
e po' 'o jolly, si 'o jolly
ce sta
e si 'o fa Pulcinella
'nduvina

B

a)

un gioco a caselle, una specie / di gioco dell'oca, sai?, / che si chiama *monapoli*: dadi / due dadi, dei dadi / indovina tu lo scopo / se hanno scopo / se arrivano alla casa con l'albero / di pino, indovina / se avanza, se indietreggia il cielo / celeste azzurrato, / se il jolly / c'è, e se lo fa / Pulcinella / indovina / indovina perché queste caselle / per metamorfosi / una scatola sono / e per il finale / ogni cosa vi salta, / vi saltano i dadi, i due dadi con lo scopo / se hanno scopo / e la casa con l'albero / di pino, e a dirotto / nella scatola il cielo / azzurrato celeste/ che indietreggi o avanzi / e poi il jolly, se il jolly / c'è / e se lo fa Pulcinella / indovina

B

a)

a game of spaces, a sort
of game of the goose, you know?,
called *monapoly*: dice
two dice, some dice
guess the purpose
if they have a purpose
if they make it to the house with the pine
tree, guess
if it goes forward, if it goes backward the sky
azured blue,
if there is
a joker, he's played by
Pulcinella
guess
guess why these spaces
morph
into a box
and in the end
everything jumps inside it,
the dice jump in it, the two dice with purpose
if they have purpose
and the house with the pine
tree, and heavy
in the box the sky
blue azured
whether moving backward or forward
and then the joker, if there is
a joker
and if he's played by Pulcinella
guess

b)

'ncopp''a periferia 'na luce lucechéa
ca pe' ssempe te sporca: te fa scampìa, fuméa

b)
sulla periferia una luce luccica / che per sempre ti sporca: ti fa terra rasa, fuliggine

b)

over the suburbs a light shines
that stains you forever: razed earth, soot

a)

nun saccio qua' sant''era, manco comme se chiammava, qua' miraculo
facette: e: dicette sant'aniello affacciànnose
'o fenestiéllo: futtìteve puverielle: e: sant'antuono
s'annammuraje d''o puorco: e: sant'uliviero sant'uliviero
ogge nunn''è comm'ajere: e: santu miserino: annure, spellate
e senza nu carlino: e: santu tischi-tosche patròne d''e
ppantòsche: e: santu mangione è nato primma 'e san giusto:
e: san callisto nun truvaje 'na rusella pe' tutt''o ciardino
'e cristo: e: san vito c''o bballo 'e san vito: e: santu martino
me mena 'nu piro, 'nu piro peracchio, 'nu cugno e 'nu cacchio, 'nu
cacchio e 'nu cugno, 'nu piro cutugno: e: tutt''e sante assieme:
oraprenobbìs:

a)
non so quale santo era, neanche come si chiamava, quale miracolo / fece: e: disse sant'aniello affacciandosi / al finestrino: / fottetevi poverelli: e: sant'antonio / s'innamorò del porco: e: sant'oliviero sant'oliviero / oggi non è come ieri: e: santo miserino: nudo, spellato / e senza un carlino: e: santo tolli-tolle patrono delle / zolle: e: santo mangione è nato prima di san giusto: / e: san callisto non trovò una rosellina in tutto il giardino / di cristo: e: san vito con il ballo di san vito: e: santo martino / mi lancia un pero, un pero peracchio, un cuneo e un cacchio, un / cacchio e un cuneo, un pero cotogno: e: tutti i santi insieme:/ orapronobis:

a)

I don't know what saint it was, his name, nor what miracle
he worked: and: sant'aniello said coming to
the window:
fuck the poor: and: sant'antonio
fell in love with the pig: and: sant'oliviero sant'oliviero
today's not like yesterday: and: santo miserino: naked, flayed
and without a penny: and: saint tin-tods patron of
clods: and: saint eats-a-lot was born before san giusto:
and: san callisto couldn't find a rosette in the whole garden
of christ: and: san vito with saint vitus dance: and: santo martino
throws me a pear tree, an ugly pear, a dick and a dare, a
dare and a dick, a quince: and: all the saints together:
orapronobis:

b)

'nu colpo 'e dadi (lettore mio ggià saje) nu levarrà
maje a miéze
'a scasualità
pure si sì deritto alleziunato strologo marpione
macchiaviéllo truttato trastulante pusato quatrato abbasato
asciutto sicco turzuto scartellato aggraziato 'mbriaco
speruto pirchio appaurato sfatecato smargiasso strampalato
'nnammuraticcio stunato scrianzato
è 'o vè'?

b)
un colpo di dadi (lettore mio già sai) non abolirà / mai / il caso / anche se sei dritto preparato astrologo marpione / machiavellico trottato trappoliere posato quadrato saggio / asciutto secco tosto gobbo aggraziato ubriaco / avido avaro impaurito sfaticato smargiasso strampalato / invaghito stonato screanzato / è cosi?

b)

a roll of the dice (as you already know my dear reader) will never abolish
chance
even if you're a shrewd unsavory astrologer machiavellian
grifter seasoned swindler poised square wise
skinny dry tough hunchback graceful drunk
greedy cheap scared lazy braggart loony
enamored spacey rude
am I right?

a)

:e: francesco cangiullo futurista
piedigrotta can-can
giullo ò scelto un nome eccentrico in anima
tissimi affiches bitter campari ecco l'omaggio
abbacinante mul
tilingue lingueggiante étoiles da concerti e la stella
cangiullo napoli
caldaia vulcanica di sismiche
folle folli che il follone
seziona con la sega - teste
all'infinito piedigrotta

a)

:and: francesco cangiullo futurist
piedigrotta can-can
giullo I chose an eccentric name from the most ani
mated affiches campari bitter here's the blinding
homage mul
tilingual tonguing concert étoiles and the star
cangiullo napoli
volcanic caldron of seismic
crazy crowds that the crusher
mangles with its jaws – heads
as far as the eye can see piedigrotta

b)

sbalanzano 'e dadi, all'alibbastro
'e 'nu bbusto svracciato ce portano: sophia
'a chiammo 'sta sfragnata
autorità : 'mmiéz"e sgarrupe,
si 'a vire, arbante juôrno, s'allima
ll'umbriccia cu 'a tranquilla
luce 'e 'nu disastro...
sophia,
ch'è 'o cchiù ggeniuso *poster*

b)
ruzzolano i dadi, all'alabastro / di un busto sbracciato ci portano: sophia / chiamo questa sbriciolata /autorità: in mezzo alle rovine, / se la vedessi, all'alba, allisciarsi / l'ombra con la tranquilla / luce di un disastro... / sophia, / che è il più sollazzevole *poster*

b)

the dice tumble, bringing us
to the alabaster of a sleeveless bust: sophia
I call on this crumbled
authority: amidst the ruins,
if you could see her, at dawn, smoothing
her shadow with the calm
light of a disaster...
sophia,
who's the most pleasing *poster*

a)

chi suppónta 'e ssuppónte d''e ssuppónte?

a)
chi puntella i puntelli dei puntelli?

a)

who's buttressing the buttresses of buttresses

b)

Ma chi è muórto?
'O pupo Stuórto.
Chi s''o porta?
'O pupo Ciorta.
Chi fa 'o taùto?
'O pupo Velluto.

b)
Ma chi è morto? / Il pupo Storto. / Chi lo porta via? / Il pupo Sorte. / Chi fa la cassa da morto? / Il pupo Velluto.

b)

who's dead
baby bent
who's carrying him up?
baby luck
who's made the coffin
baby satin

a)

le bebé, ll'ovette rutte
que se spanne dint'a ll'homme
que se spanne in hommelette

a)
il bebè, l'ovetto rotto / che si spande nell'uomo / che si spande in hommelette

a)

the baby, the broken egg
that spreads inside the homme
that spreads inside the hommelette

b)

napule addiventaje palepoli necropoli panecuócoli casaruóppoli scazzuóppoli vruóccoli ranavuóttoli spruóccoli chiéna 'e chiachiélle

b)
napoli diventò palepoli necropoli panecuocoli stambugi / pescivendoli omiciattoli broccoli ranocchi sterpi / piena di mezze calzette

b)

naples turned spadopolis necropolis panecuocoli hovels
fishmongers pipsqueaks broccolis toads brambles
filled with dimwits

a)

hadda passà' 'a chiachiellata

a)
deve passare la chiachiellata

a)

got to get through this chit-chat

b)

e tenenno 'nu nomme tipo wanda gabbriella lalla
('nu nomme 'e sociologa, 'e psicassistente sociale)
m''e 'nvitat''int'a 'st'idromassaggio - chill'uócchie
'e serpentessa arèt''e llènte a specchio (se po'?),
me lèggeno 'o ggiurnale e 'e chell'eterna
napoletanità - tu faje suspire
oj wanda gabbriella lalla, 'ncuoll'a mme
abbuccata, a mme aggranfata, e a stiénto
m'arrivano 'e pparole
napoletanità,
napolitaneria (oj wanda ca m'astrigne
'ncuórpo a tte 'o significante
ùrdemo: 'nu juóco
'mpónta 'mpónta, pe' nun farme trafficà'
pe' nun farte revistà'
e truvà') - me pare asciuta
d''o ffuto d''o medullo a vócia tója
'mpastata ca mó dice non è vero
che sia napoli il peggior di tutti i mali - oj wanda
ca faje a filologgia *dans la baignoire,*
sadica wanda-dolmancé, lalla-eugénie,
gabbriella de saint-ange, qual'alliccata
canità te porta a leggere (mentre t'è artetecuso
'o tafanario) ca fuje cu ll'atto terzo, scena terza
d' *'a cortigiana* 'e ll'aretino a primma vota

b)
e avendo un nome tipo wanda gabriella lalla / (un nome da sociologa, da psicoassistente sociale) / mi hai invitato in quest'idromassaggio -quegli occhi / di serpentessa dietro gli occhiali a specchio (si può?), / mi leggono il giornale e di quell'eterna / *napoletanità* - tu fai sospiri / o wanda gabriella lalla, su di me / piegata, a me avvinghiata, e a stento / mi arrivano le parole / *napoletanità,* / *napolitaneria* (o wanda che mi stringi / nel tuo corpo il significante / ultimo: un gioco / in punta in punta, per non farmi trafficare / per non farti rovistare / e trovare) - mi sembra uscita / dal fondo del midollo la tua voce / impastata che ora dice non è vero / che sia napoli il peggior di tutti i mali - o wanda / che fai la filologia *dans la baignoire,* / sadica wanda-dolmancé, lalla-eugénie, / gabriella de saint-ange, quale elegante / crudeltà ti porta a leggere (mentre ti è vispo / il culo) che fu con l'atto terzo, scena terza / de *la cortigiana* dell'aretino la prima volta /

b)

and having a name like wanda gabriella lalla
(a sociologist's name, a psychologist's, a social worker's)
you invited me into this jacuzzi – with eyes
snake-like behind those reflective lenses (what the hell),
they read me the paper and you turn
into sighs that eternal *neopolitanness*
oh wanda gabriella lalla, bent
over me, clinging to me, and I barely
find the words
neopolitanness,
neopolitaneity (oh wanda you're squeezing
in your body the ultimate
signifier: a game
carefully played, so I don't rummage
so I don't search you
and find) – your voice
seems to have come from the depth of your marrow
gruff as you say it's not true
that naples is the worst of evils – oh wanda
you're doing philology *dans la baignoire*,
sadistic wanda-dolmancé, lalla-eugénie,
gabriella desaint-ange, what elegant
cruelty leads you to read (while your ass
so vivacious) that it was with the third act, third scene
of aretino's *courtesian* the first time

villanella-pubblicità

'A vocca comm''a càucia, ohimé, che croce,
e 'a lengua comm''e vacca lattarola.
'A coca-cola
dint''o cannarone,
e cchiù 'e 'nu bbuttiglione
vurrìa sentirme scorrere agredóce.

'Nu senzo de cetrulo e po' de noce
cu 'o llatte de na zizza mammarola.
'A coca-cola
dint''o cannarone,
e cchiù 'e 'nu bbuttiglione,
vurrìa sentirme scorrere agredoce.

D''o zuco tuje me faccio portavoce
assaje cchiù frisco d''a vasenicòla.
'A coca-cola
dint''o cannarone,
e cchiù 'e 'nu bbuttiglione,
vurrìa sentirme scorrere agredoce.

'Nganna e 'int''o naso tu si ccellecosa,
quase comm''o ccafè miraculosa.
E si gassosa
dint''o bbicchierotto.
Qua' vino, qua' chinotto,
si p''a cannuccia saglje 'a Misteriosa?

villanella-pubblicità
La bocca come calce, ahimé, che croce, / e la lingua come di mucca lattifera. / La coca-cola / giù nel gargarozzo, / e più di un bottiglione, / vorrei sentirmi scorrere agrodolce. // Un senso di cetriolo e poi di noce / con il latte di una tetta mammarola. / La coca-cola / giù nel gargarozzo, / e più di un bottiglione, / vorrei sentirmi scorrere agrodolce. // Del succo tuo mi faccio portavoce, / molto più fresco del basilico. / La coca-cola / giù nel gargarozzo, / e più di un bottiglione, / vorrei sentirmi scorrere agrodolce. // In gola e nel naso tu sei stuzzicante, / quasi come il caffè miracolosa! / E sei gassosa / dentro il bicchierotto! / Quale vino, quale chinotto, / se su per la cannuccia sale la Misteriosa?

country girl-commercial

mouth like lime, alas, what a cross,
and a tongue like a dairy cow's,
Coca-cola
down the throat,
and more than a jug,
I'd like to feel it flow sweet and sour.

a whiff of cucumber and then walnut
with the milk from mommy's teat.
Coca-cola
down the throat,
and more than a jug,
I'd like to feel it flow sweet and sour.

I'll bear the news of your juice,
much fresher than basil.
Coca-cola
down the throat,
more than a jug,
I'd like to feel it flow sweet and sour.

In the throat and in the nose you're appetizing,
miraculous almost like coffee
you're bubbly
in the short glass!
What wine, what chinotto,
if up the straw rises the Mysterious?

'e sta parola-aggriccio: *napoletaneria*
-qua' canità
cianciosa te fa leggere *'o diario
romano* dell'imbriani, proprio 'o punto
addó dice *'nu pernacchio ci vorrebbe,
napoletanescamente* (proprio mó
ca cchiù carnale t'abbecìni) oj wanda
dolmancé, ma qua' piacere
piccante e smaliziato mó te porta
dopp'a ll'avverbio all'uso transitivo
e chistu streuzo verbo: *napoletanizzare*
('ntramente aônna e cresce 'o desiderio, e quase
è chillo 'e 'nu cucchiere): 'o viécchio fatto
'e ll'uovo e d''a gallina, se i borboni
borbonizzajeno napule o si napule 'e bborboni
napoletanizzò - po', quant'a *napoli*
comme parola nordica e smerdiante
pe' dicere 'o terrone in generale, oj lalla
gabbriella wanda, oj creola toscocalabra (ca ll'uovo
a 'a cocca indifferentemente
'o rumpe p''o culillo o 'o pizzo), quant'a *napoli,*
quant'a *napulitan,* me strilli ca nunn'era
p''e piemuntesi termine aggraziato,
mentre c'allucco basta e t'addimanno
pecché nun vuó' ca dint''a 'st'acquarella
amara 'o bastimento nuósto parte
e va a papore

di questa parola-brivido: *napoletaneria* / quale crudeltà / affettata ti fa leggere *il diario / romano* dell'imbriani, proprio nel punto / dove dice *un pernacchio ci vorrebbe,* / *napoletanescamente* (proprio ora / che più amorevole ti avvicini) o wanda / dolmancé, ma quale piacere / piccante e smaliziato ora ti porta / dopo l'avverbio all'uso transitivo / di questo strambo verbo: *napoletanizzare* / nel mentre ondeggia e cresce il desiderio, e quasi / è quello di un cocchiere): il vecchio tema / dell'uovo e della gallina, se i borboni / borbonizzarono napoli o se napoli i borboni / *napoletanizzò* - poi, quanto a *napoli,* / come parola nordica e smerdante / per dire il terrone in generale, o lalla / gabbriella wanda, o creola toscocalabra (che l'uovo / à la coque indifferentemente / rompi dal culetto o dalla sommità), quanto a *napoli,* / quanto a *napoletano,* mi strilli che non era / per i piemontesi termine aggraziato, / mentre grido basta e ti domando / perché non vuoi che in quest'acquetta / amara il bastimento nostro parta / e vada a vapore

of this word-shiver: *neopolitanness*
- what affected
cruelty makes you read the *roman
diary* by imbriani, right the passage
where he says *that really calls for a raspberry*,
neopolitanesquely (right now
as you approach most lovingly) oh wanda
dolmancé, but what spicy
shrewd pleasure now takes you
after the adverb to a transitive usage
of this odd verb: *neopolitanize*
(whilst the desire sways and grows, and it's almost
that of a coachman): the old theme
of the chicken and the egg, if the bourbons
bourbonized naples or if naples *napolitanized*
the bourbons - then, as for *naples*,
like a northern shit slinging word
to mean southerner in general,
or lalla
gabriella wanda, or creole tosco-calabrese (for you break
the egg à la coque indifferently
at the heinie or on the top), as for *naples*,
as for *neopolitan*, you yell at me that it wasn't
for the piedmontese a graceful term,
while I yell to you enough and I ask you
why you don't want in this little bitter
water our freighter to leave and steam away

B

a)
io faccio marat, tu faje carlotta
corday? a turno?

B
a)
io faccio marat, tu fai carlotta / corday? a turno?

B)

a)
I do marat, you do carlotta,
corday? we take turns?

b)

'o super-io 'e napule: milano

b)
il super-io di napoli: milano

b)

naples super-ego: milan

De comendatione
Mediolani ratione habitantium

Ratione habitantium considerata...
Si vulimmo 'uardà 'a ggente, io Milano
'a veco 'a cchiù bbella d'"e ccittà d'"o munno.
Comm'infatti 'a ggente 'e llà só' jiuste
comm'altezza, uómmene e femmene;
allère 'e faccia, abbastanzamente
'e core; nun 'mbrogliano, nun teneno
malizia cu 'e furastiere, e pe' cchesto
'e ggente 'e ssanno arricunoscere
mmiez'a ll'ati ggente. Càmpano
commilfó, sanno 'a crianza 'o sòrdo
assignatezza, se mettono panni ca fanno
onore; 'a casa lloro o fora, addó se trovano
só' abbastanzamente sciampagnune
quanno spenneno,
apprezzano e só' apprezzate, sanno ausà
bbonamaniera dint'"a vita. E comme
'a lengua ca parlano è 'a lengua
ca 'mmiez'a ll'ate se parla
e se capisce meglio, accussì pure lloro
subbet'"e ccunusce, 'mmiez'a chi sia sia:
bast'"a presenza! Song' o no,
cchiù 'e tutte quante, chille
ca s'hann'a rispettà'?

Elogio / di Milano per i suoi abitanti
Ratione habitantium considerata... / Considerata in rapporto ai suoi abitanti, Milano / mi sembra la più bella città del mondo. / Infatti i nativi di Milano sono di giusta / statura, uomini e donne; / di aspetto sorridente, piuttosto / benevoli; non ingannano, non usano / malizia con i forestieri, e per questo / sono distinguibili più degli altri / fra le restanti genti. Vivono / come si deve, conoscono la creanza il denaro / l'avvedutezza, indossano vesti / onorevoli; in patria e fuori, dovunque si trovino / sono piuttosto liberi / nello spendere, / apprezzano e vengono apprezzati, sanno usare / urbani modi nel vivere. E come / l'idioma che parlano è l'idioma / che fra gli altri si parla / e si capisce meglio, così essi stessi / li riconosci subito, tra qualsiasi gente: / dal solo loro aspetto! Non sono dunque, / tra tutte le genti, quelli / più degni di stima?

De comendatione
Mediolani ratione habitantium

Ratione habitantium considerata...
If considered in relation to its inhabitants, Milan
seems to me the most beautiful city in the world.
In fact Milan's natives are the right
height, both men and women;
of a smiling appearance, rather
benevolent; they don't deceive, they show
no malice toward foreigners, and for this reason
are the most distinguished of all other
remaining peoples. They live
as one should, they know propriety money
prudence, they wear honorable
clothing; at home and abroad, wherever they may be
they're quite liberal
in spending,
they appreciate and are appreciated, they display
urban manners in their lives. And as
their language out of all
the others is the easiest
to speak and understand, so are they themselves
immediately recognizable no matter who's around them:
one need only look at them! Aren't they, then,
out of all peoples, those
most deserving of our esteem?

a)

jettàto 'a mmiézejuôrno 'int"a 'nu scàrrafo ggiallo (vecchia razza
'e ferraglia 'o trambùs, arrecatta
ggente e ggenimme spartùte, c'arrasso
se tèneno, c'aumbróse
scunfîdano una 'e 'n'ata, comm"e tutta
'a suggetà), nun m'arritrovo
'mmiéz'a 'mbrugliuso 'mbruóglio? nun richiama
nu sbafantóne cuolloluóngo c"o cappiéllo a viaggiatore
scunusciuto pe' fesseria 'e cafè? Ué, nun s"a piglia
'a quistione
p"o dito gruósso d"o père scarpesato?
S"a piglia! se 'ngrifa, bbell'e bbuóno faccetuósto, cu 'o pparlà'
ca se spannètte niro niro
'e 'ncucciamiénto... ìh-comme
stévemo 'int"a chillu trambùs (me s'agghiurdava
'a mente, ué, pròpeto comm"a pelle, pecché niente
cchiù d"a paura fa paura): ìh che strèuzo
e buriuso 'o 'uaglione, ca pe' fforza
se vuleva appiccecà' cu' 'nu bbell'ommo (ddì' 'e cliente
'stu 'uaglione, diceva
ch'era stato 'ntuppato): ma nun saccio chi era, chi fuje: stéve sotto
'o cappiéllo a ddôje pónte a tre pónte a tre acque
a tre vviénte a piuppino a lucerna a sombrero a cappuccio
a turbante a pileo a gibùs a képì: me pareva
curiuso 'o cappiéllo d"o 'nzisto

a)
gettato a mezzogiorno in uno scarafaggio giallo (vecchi razza / di ferraglia il trambus, raccoglie / gente e genie separate, che lontane / si tengono, che ombrose / diffidano una dell'altra, come di tutta / la società), non mi ritrovo / in mezzo a un complicato imbroglio? non fa una partaccia / un fanfarone collolungo col cappello a viaggiatore / sconosciuto per un'inezia? Ué, non attacca / briga / per l'alluce calpestato? / La attacca! s'impenna, all'improvviso facciatosta, con il parlare / che si diffuse nero nero / di ostinazione... ah, come / stavamo in quel trambus (mi si aggricciava / la mente, ué, proprio come la pelle, perché niente / più della paura fa paura): a che strambo / e borioso il ragazzo, che a forza / voleva litigare con un tizio (che cliente / 'sto ragazzo, diceva / ch'era stato sfiorato): ma non so chi era, chi fu: stava sotto / il cappello a due punte a tre punte a tre acque / a tre venti a pioppino a lucerna a sombrero a cappuccio / a turbante a pileo a gibùs a képì: mi sembrava / strano il cappello del bravaccio

a)

thrown at midday into a yellow cockroach (a kind of old pile
of scrap metal the trolley bus, collecting
peoples and various races, who keep
apart, who are sullen
and mistrust each other, as well as all of
society), do I find myself
in the middle of a complex scheme? does a long-neck loudmouth
sporting a hat berate a strange
traveler over a trifle? Ohi, isn't he getting
all worked up
over a stepped-on toe?
You bet he does! He raises, suddenly the brazen-faced, his speech
that propagates pitch-black
with stubbornness... oh, how
we were on that trolley bus (my mind
shriveled, ohi, just like skin, for nothing
is more frightful than fright): oh how bizarre
and pompous that boy, who insisted
on picking a fight with that fellow (what a customer
this boy, he said
having been grazed): but I don't know who he was, who he used to be: he
                                                                                                was hiding
under a hat with two brims three brims three waters
three winds a pork pie a bucket a sombrero a hood
a turban a pileus a gibus a kepi: it looked strange that thug's hat

b)

napule
(e 'e trentasei casale): panza
dint''a panza
d''a nazióne (bbusillo e bbuco niro
dint''o tarallóne)

b)
napoli / (e i trentasei casali): ventre / nel ventre / della nazione (busillis e buco nero / nel ciambellone)

b)

naples
(and its thirty six casali): belly
within the belly
of the nation (blight and black hole
in the donut)

a)

chiossà' ca 'nce serpiava d' afflittivo, 'e stupetiàto
'int''a voce d''o psichiatra pe' ttramente
murmuriava : " 'a fantasia d''o criaturo cu 'mmano
'a mmerda pe' marènna è 'o munno,
'o stranizzato 'nfame munno" e all'intrasatto
'nu stucchio d'ache s'agliuttètte, e strafalàrio
cchiù nunn'era 'e faccia, e cchiù nunn'era
'a faccia 'e 'n'astròloco, 'int''a ll'ùrdemo
sùscio, addó diceva: "'o nniénte
m''o ffacc'io, m''o vvoglio dà'
a ppe' mme"

a)
chissà cosa vi strisciava di afflittivo, di imbambolato / nella voce dello psichiatra nel mentre / mormorava: "la fantasia del bambino con in mano / la merda per merenda è il mondo, / lo stranizzato infame mondo" e all'improvviso / un astuccio d'aghi inghiottì, e perdigiorno / più non era in viso, e più non era / il viso di un astrologo, nell'ultimo / soffio, in cui diceva: "il niente / me lo faccio io, voglio darmelo / da me"

a)

who knows what sort of affliction, of astonishment slithered
in the psychiatrist's voice as he
whispered: "the fantasy of the child holding
a turd as if it were a snack is the world,
the bewildered vile world" and suddenly
he swallowed a small case filled with needles and his face
no longer looked like that of an idler, nor was it an astrologist's
face, with his last
breath he said: "I'll make
my own nothing, I'll get it
myself"

A
b)

s'arrapa a *rap*,
'nu picchio niro: 'o ritmo
pare s'arape

A
b)
s'arrapa a *rap*, / un picchio nero: il ritmo / pare si apra

A
b)

he's getting randy *rapping*,
a black wood pecker: the rhythm
appears to open

a)

grazia e valore ancora se vedeno:
'na partita 'e pallone fra 'uagliùne, specie chillo,
'o vì, ca joca all'ala, vola
'ncopp''o cuórpo tìseco d''a piazza...
tuórno tuórno grattaciéle: malómbre
curiose: culonne
'e 'nu ddio sulitario? ('nu ddio
ca prutegge rendite? 'uaragne?)

ccà metropoli e folla
fann''o tiatro d''e ccose
perfette?

'na serpe se magna stess'essa, se mózzeca
'a cora 'nzevata
'e menuzzaglia umana?

'n'alieno?

qua' spirale s'attorce
dint''a 'stu fravecà' ggigantizzato
pe' ll'ommo-póllece?

a)
grazia e valore ancora si vedono: / una partita di pallone fra ragazzi, specie quello, / vedi che gioca all'ala, vola / sul corpo rigido della piazza... / attorno attorno grattacieli: malombre / strane: colonne / di un dio solitario? / (un dio / che protegge rendite? guadagni?) // qui metropoli e folla / fanno il teatro delle cose / perfette? // un serpente mangia sé stesso, si morde / la coda unta / di minutaglia umana? // un alieno? // quale spirale si attorce / in un fabbricare gigantizzato / per l'uomo-pulce?

a)

grace and valor can still be seen:
a ball game among kids, especially that,
you see the one playing on the wing, he's flying
on the taut body of the square...
skyscrapers all around: strange
evil shadows: columns
of a solitary god?
(a god
who protects returns? profits?)

here metropolis and crowds
comprise the theater of perfect
things?

a serpent eating itself, biting its own
greasy tail
of human bric-a-brac?

an alien?

what spiral coils
in a giganticized manufacturing
for the lice-man?

villanella-pubblicità

'A vocca comm"a càucia, ohimé, che croce,
e 'a lengua comm"e vacca lattarola.
'A coca-cola
dint"o cannarone,
e cchiù 'e 'nu bbuttiglione
vurrìa sentirme scorrere agredóce.

'Nu senzo de cetrulo e po' de noce
cu 'o llatte de na zizza mammarola.
'A coca-cola
dint"o cannarone,
e cchiù 'e 'nu bbuttiglione,
vurrìa sentirme scorrere agredoce.

D"o zuco tuje me faccio portavoce
assaje cchiù frisco d"a vasenicòla.
'A coca-cola
dint"o cannarone,
e cchiù 'e 'nu bbuttiglione,
vurrìa sentirme scorrere agredoce.

'Nganna e 'int"o naso tu si ccellecosa,
quase comm"o ccafè miraculosa.
E si gassosa
dint"o bbicchierotto.
Qua' vino, qua' chinotto,
si p"a cannuccia saglje 'a Misteriosa?

villanella-pubblicità
La bocca come calce, ahimé, che croce, / e la lingua come di mucca lattifera. / La coca-cola / giù nel gargarozzo, / e più di un bottiglione, / vorrei sentirmi scorrere agrodolce. // Un senso di cetriolo e poi di noce / con il latte di una tetta mammarola. / La coca-cola / giù nel gargarozzo, / e più di un bottiglione, / vorrei sentirmi scorrere agrodolce. // Del succo tuo mi faccio portavoce, / molto più fresco del basilico. / La coca-cola / giù nel gargarozzo, / e più di un bottiglione, / vorrei sentirmi scorrere agrodolce. // In gola e nel naso tu sei stuzzicante, / quasi come il caffè miracolosa! / E sei gassosa / dentro il bicchierotto! / Quale vino, quale chinotto, / se su per la cannuccia sale la Misteriosa?

country girl-commercial

mouth like lime, alas, what a cross,
and a tongue like a dairy cow's,
Coca-cola
down the throat,
and more than a jug,
I'd like to feel it flow sweet and sour.

a whiff of cucumber and then walnut
with the milk from mommy's teat.
Coca-cola
down the throat,
and more than a jug,
I'd like to feel it flow sweet and sour.

I'll bear the news of your juice,
much fresher than basil.
Coca-cola
down the throat,
more than a jug,
I'd like to feel it flow sweet and sour.

In the throat and in the nose you're appetizing,
miraculous almost like coffee
you're bubbly
in the short glass!
What wine, what chinotto,
if up the straw rises the Mysterious?

gulliver?

le roi nous fit proposer de venir voir,
à un des balcons de son palais,
l'une de fêtes les plus singulières de son royaume...
il s'agissait d'un cocagne

cuccagna?

furmiculìo d''a folla? stesa 'e paura senza nomme
'int''a 'nu spazio addó se schiéja 'n'assurdo?

si vous ne connaissez pas ce spectacle
nous dit le roi
vous allez le trouver bien barbare

sta disturbato 'stu spazio? e che cuncertano
'sti scatulune mai allerchìni mai
pullecenella?
(maimai 'nu poco bbuffune, ma che tèneno
'na maschera scuièta 'e chiarità, senza 'na fistula,
'na canniatura...)

gulliver? // *le roi nous fit proposer de venir voir,* / *à un des balcons de son palais,* / *l'une de fêtes les plus singulières de son royaume...* / *il s'agissait d'un cocagne* // cuccagna? // formicolìo della folla? distesa di paura senza nome / in uno spazio dove si distende un assurdo? // *si vous ne connaissez pas ce spectacle* / *nous dit le roi* / *vous allez le trouver bien barbare* // è disturbato questo spazio? e cosa concertano // questi scatoloni mai arlecchini mai / pulcinella? / (maimai un po' buffoni, ma che hanno / una maschera inquieta di chiarità / senza una fistola / una fenditura...) //

gulliver?

*le roi nous fit proposer de venir voir,
à un des balcons de son palais,
l'une de fêtes les plus singulières de son royaume...
il s'agissait d'un cocagne*

cockange?

the crowds teeming? expanse of nameless fear
in a space where the absurd unravels?

*si vous ne connaissez pas ce spectacle
nous dit le roi
vous allez le trouver bien barbare*

is this space disturbed? and what do you make
of these boxes never arlequins never
pulcinellas?
(nevernever a bit fools, but wearing
a disquieting mask of clarity
without a fistula
without an opening...)

'a città sparisce
'int"a 'nu viavai
'e ggente ch'è sparita?

scuncecato è 'stu spazio?

sur un grand échafaud galline e papere
'nchiuvate, mise 'ncroce p' 'o spasso d' 'o popolo

des pièces de toile disposées de manière
à former les flots de la mer

'e spazzie apiérte se só ammattugliate? 'n'allucco
nunn' asciùto 'stu spazio?
foglie secche 'ntrucchiate
'e spazzie 'e tutte quante?

'nu spazio privato e annascuso s'aggliuttètte
cantastorie
musicanti
magnafuoco
filastrocche tiritère stroppule
rocchie 'e ggente?

'o *genius loci*, 'o ggeniuslò (o comme se chiamma
'o penziero, 'a voglia 'e dicere 'e 'nu posto): tutto sfriddo?
manco ll'uósemo?

telle est... l'amorce...'a trappula appriparata...
...un second coup de canon se fit entendre...

la città sparisce / in un viavai / di gente che è sparita ? // guastato è questo spazio? // *sur un grand échafaud galline e papere / inchiodate, messe in croce per lo spasso del popolo // des pièces de toile disposées de manière / à former les flots de la mer //* gli spazi aperti si sono ammassati? un urlo / non emesso questo spazio? / foglie secche accartocciate / gli spazi di tutti? // uno spazio privato e nascosto inghiottì / cantastorie / musici / mangiafuoco / filastrocche tiritere scherzi // capannelli di gente? // il *genius loci*, il geniuslò (o come si chiama / il pensiero, il- voler-dire di un luogo): tutto scarto? / nemmeno l'odore? // *telle est... l'amorce... la trappula preparata.../ un second coup de canon se fit entendre...//*

the city disappears
in the comings and goings
of people who disappeared?

the space ruined?

*sur un grand échafaud galline e papere
'nchiuvate, mise 'ncroce p' 'o spasso d' 'o popolo*

*des pièces de toile disposées de manière
à former les flots de la mer*

the open spaces bunched up? a scream
that didn't emerge this space?
dead crumbled leaves
everyone's spaces?

a private and hidden space swallowed
storytellers
musicians
fire-eaters
nursery rhymes lullabies jokes
knots of people?

the *genius loci*, the geniuslò (or whatever it's called
a place's thought, intent-to-speak): all scraps?
Not even the smell?

*telle est... l'amorce... a trap set...
...un second coup de canon se fit entendre...*

sottoterra ? senza cielo 'e ppiazze, senza
assaggià' decidere vedé'?
e 'nu spazio pe' sbià' fore
ll'istinto 'e arricettarse?

'o ffore, 'o ddinto
nun se parlano cchiù 'e niente?

sottoterra? senza cielo le piazze, senza / assaggiare decidere vedere? / e uno spazio per sviare fuori / l'istinto di uccidersi? // il fuori, il dentro / non si parlano più di niente?

underground?
without sky squares, without
tasting deciding seeing?
and a space for deflecting outward
the instinct to kill one's self?

the outside, the inside
they don't speak about anything anymore?

b)

ferdinando
io, ccioè nuje, ferdinando... (che nummero tengo... tenimmo
mò?)
che songo, che simmo? IV?
o I?
III?
vabbuó... ferdinando! 'o rre (pe' grazzia
'e ddio) d"e ddôje sicilie ddôje,
'e gerusalemme (vabbuó...),
infante 'e spagna &cc.
duca 'e parma, piacenza, castro &cc. &cc.,
principe ereditiero (ereditario?) d"a tuscana &cc. &cc. &cc.,
faccio (o facimmo?) un bando, a dì vinte 'e settembre
1789,
eh! sì! poco doppo
c"a ggente 'e miez"a via, 'a zandragliarìa,
ha fatto chillu scassascassa c"a bbastiglia
vabbuó?
e facimmo (o faccio?) 'stu bbando pecché nun saccio pecché
dopp"ammuìna 'e pariggi,
'o cielo 'e napule è chino 'e pallune,
'e mungulfiere smargiasse...
e io...
nuje...
ìennuje!
facciofacimmo 'o bbando!
puff!
sgonfiosgunfiammo
'stu cielo chino 'e bbolle d'aria
vabbuó?
pecché capruscellano a ccratèrio 'ncopp"o cranio mio
sti muschille
ronzano a saetta a salata a sagljescìnne
spalommano spaccunciélle 'int"a 'na spaccunata
só' frizzante

b)

f e r d i n a n d o
I, that is we, ferdinando… (what number am I… are we now?)
what am I, what are we? IV?
Or I?
III?
oh well… ferdinando! the king (by the grace
of god) of the two sicilies two,
of jerusalem (oh well),
infant of spain &cc.
duke of parma, piacenza, castro &cc. &cc.,
issue (or we issue?) a decree, this twentieth of september
1789,
eh! yes! right after
the people in the streets, the rubble
has done all that smash and grab with the bastille
right?
we issue (or I issue?) this decree because I don't know why
after all that noise in paris,
the sky of naples is full of balloons,
of braggart hot air balloons…
and I…
we…
weandI!
Iissueweissue this decree!
puff!
Ideflatewedeflate
the sky full of air bubbles
right?
because they're goating like craters on my skull
these fruit flies
buzzing like a flash like a brine like a latch
fluttering about like a boaster in braggadocio
they sparkle
they mock humming like flies

sfruculéjeno a turdiglione muschìto
a zurre-zurre
aucelléano a trapano
runzéano a fisce-fisce a murmurizzo
pissi-pissi vociavòcio vesbiglio 'e z
z
zunzuléjeno dint''e rrecchie stennécchiano e stizzano
'e nierve
sturzellano
fanno 'e 'sta cuntrora 'nu sfarenamiénto
'stu bbellu cielo azzurro ll'aùsano, chiassùse,
pe' ffa' 'na iacuvella 'nu sfottò: cucù

b)
io, cioè noi, ferdinando... (che numero ho... abbiamo / adesso?) / che sono, che siamo? IV? / o I? / III? / vabbè... ferdinando! il re (per grazia / di dio) delle due sicilie due, / di gerusalemme (vabbè), / infante di spagna &cc. / duca di parma, piacenza, castro &cc. &cc., / faccio (o facciamo?) un bando, addì venti di settembre / 1789, / eh! sì! poco dopo / che la gente di strada, la plebaglia / ha fatto quel rompirompi con la bastiglia / va bene? / e facciamo (o faccio?) questo bando perché non so perché / dopo il chiasso di parigi, / il cielo di napoli è pieno di palloni, / di mongolfiere sbruffone... / e io... / noi... / ioennoi! / facciofacciamo il bando! / puff! / sgonfiosgonfiamo / questo cielo pieno di bolle d'aria / vabbè? / perché capretteggiano a cratere sul mio cranio / questi moscerini / ronzano a saetta a salata a saliscendi / sfarfallano spacconcelli in una spacconata / sono frizzanti / sfottono a ronzìo di mosca / a bzz bzz / girano a trapano / ronzano a fss fss a mormorio / pissi-pissi vocìo bisbiglìo di z / z / zanzareggiano nelle orecchie strizzano e stizzano / i nervi / indispongono / fanno di questo pisolo uno sfarinamento / questo bel cielo azzurro lo usano, chiassosi / per fare una camarilla uno sfottò : cucù

like bzz bzz
they turn like a drill
buzzing like fss fss like a whisper
pissi-pissi clamoring murmuring of z
z
mosquitoing in the ears they upset and unsettle
the nerves
they distress
they turn this nap into an erosion
this beautiful blue sky they use it, rowdy
to form a camarilla a joke: peek-a-boo

villanella-pubblicità

'A vocca comm''a càucia, ohimé, che croce,
e 'a lengua comm''e vacca lattarola.
'A coca-cola
dint''o cannarone,
e cchiù 'e 'nu bbuttiglione
vurrìa sentirme scorrere agredóce.

'Nu senzo de cetrulo e po' de noce
cu 'o llatte de na zizza mammarola.
'A coca-cola
dint''o cannarone,
e cchiù 'e 'nu bbuttiglione,
vurrìa sentirme scorrere agredoce.

D''o zuco tuje me faccio portavoce
assaje cchiù frisco d''a vasenicòla.
'A coca-cola
dint''o cannarone,
e cchiù 'e 'nu bbuttiglione,
vurrìa sentirme scorrere agredoce.

'Nganna e 'int''o naso tu si ccellecosa,
quase comm''o ccafè miraculosa.
E si gassosa
dint''o bbicchierotto.
Qua' vino, qua' chinotto,
si p''a cannuccia saglje 'a Misteriosa?

villanella-pubblicità
La bocca come calce, ahimé, che croce, / e la lingua come di mucca lattifera. / La coca-cola / giù nel gargarozzo, / e più di un bottiglione, / vorrei sentirmi scorrere agrodolce. // Un senso di cetriolo e poi di noce / con il latte di una tetta mammarola. / La coca-cola / giù nel gargarozzo, / e più di un bottiglione, / vorrei sentirmi scorrere agrodolce. // Del succo tuo mi faccio portavoce, / molto più fresco del basilico. / La coca-cola / giù nel gargarozzo, / e più di un bottiglione, / vorrei sentirmi scorrere agrodolce. // In gola e nel naso tu sei stuzzicante, / quasi come il caffè miracolosa! / E sei gassosa / dentro il bicchierotto! / Quale vino, quale chinotto, / se su per la cannuccia sale la Misteriosa?

country girl-commercial

mouth like lime, alas, what a cross,
and a tongue like a dairy cow's,
Coca-cola
down the throat,
and more than a jug,
I'd like to feel it flow sweet and sour.

a whiff of cucumber and then walnut
with the milk from mommy's teat.
Coca-cola
down the throat,
and more than a jug,
I'd like to feel it flow sweet and sour.

I'll bear the news of your juice,
much fresher than basil.
Coca-cola
down the throat,
more than a jug,
I'd like to feel it flow sweet and sour.

In the throat and in the nose you're appetizing,
miraculous almost like coffee
you're bubbly
in the short glass!
What wine, what chinotto,
if up the straw rises the Mysterious?

cucù...
e col presente bbando
ordinordinammo a tutte quante
(ai nobbili sott"a pena 'e 5 anne
d'esilio;
agl'ignobbili sott"a pena 'e 5 anne
'e galera: cinche e cinche: pe' ggiustizia)
'e nun mannà' p"o cielo 'e napule
pallune a ffuoco...
e 'stu bbando, stu cumanno reale
vogliovulìmmo ca vène sprubbecàto
e strummettiàto (c"a trumbetta bbona)
accussì niente scuse
po'
ca nisciuno 'o ssapeva
:ué: 'a legge
'a legge
nunn'ammette ignorantità

cucù... / e col presente bando /ordinordiniamo a tutti / (ai nobili sotto pena di 5 anni / di esilio; / agl'ignobili sotto pena di 5 anni / di galera: cinque e cinque: per giustizia) / di non mandare su per il cielo di napoli / palloni a fuoco... / e questo bando, questo comando reale / vogliovogliamo che venga reso pubblico / e strombazzato (con la trombetta buona) / così niente scuse / poi / che nessuno sapeva /:ué: la legge / la legge / non ammette ignoranza

peek-a-boo...
and with the present decree
Iorderweorder all
(to the noblemen under penalty of 5 years
in exile;
to the plebes under penalty of 5 years
in prison: five and five: to be fair)
not to send up in the sky of naples
fire balloons...
and this decree, this royal command
Iwantwewant it to be made public
and tooted (on the good trumpet)
so there are no excuses
later on
that people didn't know
:ohi: the law
the law
ignorance is no excuse

a)

quantos per Napolim fallitos cerno barones

a)
quanti baroni falliti vedo per napoli

a)

quantos per Napolim fallitos cerno barones

b)

"*this horrible but superb painting*", primmo verso
'e 'na poesia 'e william carlos williams
ca se chiamma *'o paraustiello d"e cecate*, poesia
'ncopp"o quadro ca pittaje pieter bruegel: 'na chiórma
'e pezziente cecate (magnifico
quadro e terribbele, astipato
a ccapemonte a nnapule)
'e senz'uócchie
se portano uno cu 'n'ato (io te tengo,
tiéneme), 'e traviérzo
 pe' ddint"o disegno 'nzin"o bbutto, 'nzino
'o fuósso d'acqua cheta, 'mpantanata
'int"a 'na forma ca va contr"e spazzie
amice e ammesurate... e 'sti ssequènzie
d'esistenze vèneno vanno
un'appriéss'a 'n'ata se vóttano se squagliano
cu 'a linea deritta ca disegnano, grado dopp'a ggrado, ma nun tène
eco pe' ll'uocchie, rima
pe' 'na f ï ura manco 'o passo
ca move comm'a llônna
 o c'a 'nu capo
a 'n'ato zumpuléa : sempe se spanne
'ncatarattato silenzio d"o nido
muorto d"e vvìsciule, sempe
niro ll'arazzo, 'a tela ca s'allonga
fra 'a 'uardàta e chi 'uarda

b)

«*quest'orribile ma superbo quadro*», primo verso / di una poesia di william carlos williams / che si chiama *la parabola dei ciechi*, poesia / sul quadro che dipinse pieter bruegel: un gruppo / di straccioni ciechi (magnifico / quadro e terribile, conservato / a capodimonte a napoli) / i senza occhi / si sorreggono uno con l'altro (io ti tengo / tienimi), di traverso / per il disegno, fino alla caduta, fino / al fosso d'acqua cheta, impantanata / in una forma che va contro gli spazi / amici e misurati... e queste sequenze / di esistenze vengono vanno / una dietro l'altra si spingono si squagliano / con la linea diritta che disegnano, grado dopo grado, ma non ha / eco per gli occhi, rima / per un'immagine neanche il passo / che muove come l'onda / o che da un capo / all'altro saltella: sempre si spande / cieco silenzio dal nido / morto delle pupille, sempre / nero l'arazzo, la tela che si allunga / fra lo sguardo e chi guarda

b)

"*this horrible but superb painting,*" first verse
of a poem by william carlos williams
entitled *the parable of the blind*, a poem
about the painting by pieter bruegel: a group
of blind beggars (magnificent
and terrible painting, housed
at capodimonte in naples)
the eyeless
hold each other up (wobbly
on their feet), diagonally
across the frame, all the way to their fall, up
to the ditch filled with still water, muddy
in a shape that goes against the friendly
and measured spaces… and these sequences
of existences come and go
one after the other they push they dissolve
into the straight line they trace, step after step, but there's no
echo for the eyes, no rhyme
for an image not even the pace
that moves forward like a wave
or that jumps
from one end to the other: ever expanding
blind silence from the dead
nest of the pupils, forever
black the tapestry, the canvas stretching
between gaze and onlooker

B

b)

tutt''o disegno fuje a criterio greco
'int''e vvie 'e napule, addó ll'angele e 'e sante
a pprimma matina piglian' 'a rincorsa
pe' puté' stà' ferme tutt''a santa jurnata,
jurnata ca po' aràpeno, a fforza, quann'è 'a sera,
comm''a 'na cozza, 'n'ostrica: scanagliano
si 'nu poco, si ammacàri
'nu poco 'e presenza salvatrice o ausiliatrice
ll'hanno tenuta 'mmiéz''e vvie - ma sempe chiùreno
'e scatto, védeno quaccosa
ca pe' lloro è comm''a A c''o chirchio attuórno, cu ll'aureola
soccia 'a lloro - ih comme 'nzerrano
'e tutta 'na città 'a jastémma forte
o chella calma, 'o ssà'?, ca truóve mmiez'a ll'uócchio d''o ciclone
ca porta cose a scuónceco, 'spartate e a scaso

b)
tutto il disegno fu a criterio greco / nelle vie di napoli, dove gli angeli e i santi / di primo mattino prendono la rincorsa / per restare fermi tutta la santa giornata, / giornata che poi aprono, a forza, quando è sera, / come una cozza, un'ostrica: scandagliano / se un poco, se magari / un poco di presenza salvatrice o ausiliatrice / l'hanno assicurata nelle strade -ma sempre chiudono / di scatto, vedono qualcosa / che per loro è come la A con il cerchio attorno, con l'aureola / simile alla loro - ah come serrano / di tutta una città la bestemmia forte / o quella calma, sai?, che trovi in mezzo all'occhio del ciclone / che porta cose alla rinfusa, isolate e casuali

B)

b)

the whole plan was done according to a Greek design
in the streets of naples, where angels and saints
early in the morning take a run up
to keep still the whole day,
a day which they force open, in the evening,
as if it were a mussel an oyster: they probe it
to see if there might be a bit
of that saving or aiding presence
they left in the street – but they always snap it
closed as they see something
that to them is like the A surrounded by a circle, like a halo
similar to theirs – oh how they shut
the strong blasphemy of the entire city
or the quiet one, you know?, that you can find in the eye of the storm
that carries a jumble of things, isolated and random

a)

e chesta nova
sfessazione poetica p''e 2
, 5 lettori 'na zinèfra ancora
vo' fa', spàrpeta 'n'ùrdemo
cerefuóglio
e po' fernesce

a)
e questa nuova / miseria poetica per i 2 / , 5 lettori un fregio ancora / vuole fare, freme un ultimo / ghirigoro / e poi finisce

a)

and this new
poetic misery still wants to provide for the 2
, 5 readers
another frieze, one last
flourish
and then it ends

Da PINOCCHIO (MOVIOLE)

From PINOCCHIO (REPLAYS)

del proprio amore innamorati,
ancora e sempre
come nei primi quindici minuti
di pubertà, si disorientano
pinocchi
e pinocchie l'un l'altro, si frastornano
a bugie così feconde che una sola
ne partorisce cento

hanno sensi di colpa
pinocchi
e pinocchie, paure,
segreti e cercano distanze

cercano vicinanze
pinocchi e pinocchie con fame
d'intimità

possono dire
ogni cosa, ogni cosa
va in una
delle due direzioni dell'ansia

parole
incredute, esaurite
sostanze in un gioco di soffi
vuoti di favella

in love with one's own love,
again and forever
like in the first fifteen minutes
of puberty, pinocchios
and she pinocchios
baffle each other, bamboozle
each other with lies so fertile that one
alone births a hundred

they feel guilty
pinocchios and
she pinocchios, afraid,
secretive and seek distance

they seek closeness
pinocchios and she pinocchios hungry
for intimacy

they can say
anything, everything
goes in one
of the two directions of angst

words
unbelieved, exhausted
substances in a game of puffs
emptied of speech

Da Pinocchio (moviole)

parole
mai dette, sospese
in un sonno
di pipistrelli

bugie,
gambe corte e lunghissime
braccia che raggiungono
il remoto delle emozioni

con foglie di fico, fra angosce
di trasparenza celano i bugiardi
pinocchi e pinocchie antiche piaghe,
i loro acuti neri

nutrono fole
con circuìta, divisa
verità
o moltiplicata – fole
con occhi densi di cielo
fatte bere,
a non amare golate

agili
al ricamo del mentire pinocchi
e pinocchie creano sfilze
di cose in cui le vere riflettono

words
never spoken, suspended
in a bat's
slumber

lies,
short legs and very long
arms that reach
the farthest of emotions

with fig leaves, between anguishes
of transparency hide ancient
sores the lying pinocchios and she pinocchios,
their black high notes

nourish fabrications
with circumvented, divided
truth
or multiplied – fabrications
with sky-dense eyes
made to drink,
in unbitter gulps

quick
to the call
of deceit pinocchios
and she pinocchios
create scores
of things where truth reflects

luce fidata sulle false

pinocchi e pinocchie che diventano
gelosi
e dipendenti come quelli,
tutti quelli a cui si mente,
delicati
e paranoici – a volte
non credono al vero

per sé una faccia,
una
per l'altro diventato
all'infinito interprete

le viscere
soltanto, le indovine,
in notti chimiche,
in fiele, fanno vana
ogni fatica d'invenzione

non giungono per poco
al nome nuovo
annidato nell'altro

its trusted light on fiction

pinocchios and she pinocchios that grow
jealous
and clingy like those,
all those to whom one lies,
delicate and paranoid – at times
they don't believe the truth

one face for themselves,
one
for the other they become
actors for the rest of time

the viscera
alone, the soothsayers,
over chemical nights,
the gall, foil
any attempt at invention

they almost reach
the new name
nestled in the other

www.ingramcontent.com/pod-product-compliance
Lightning Source LLC
Chambersburg PA
CBHW030054100526
44591CB00008B/145